★★★★ Civil War ★★★★
Ghosts
at
Fort Delaware

HISTORY, MYSTERY, LEGEND AND LORE

Stories and Photographs by

Ed Okonowicz

Civil War Ghosts at Fort Delaware
First Edition

ISBN 1-890690-16-3

Published by
Myst and Lace Publishers, Inc.
1386 Fair Hill Lane
Elkton, Maryland 21921

Printed in the U.S.A.
in Baltimore, Maryland
by Victor Graphics

Typography, Layout and Cover Design
by Kathleen Okonowicz

Cover photographs, clockwise, from top:
Fort Delaware, from the southeast,
re-enactor Willis Phelps Jr. at a Civil War gravesite, and
the interior Parade Ground of the fort.

Dedications

To Audrey, Adam and Dru
Welcome to the family.
Ed Okonowicz

Acknowledgments

The author and illustrator appreciate the assistance of those
who have played an important role in this project.

For providing access to the sites, taking the time to be interviewed
and providing photographs and information: Carla Anderson,
Rev. Gary Baer, Alfred Bestwick, Dale Fetzer, Donna Bowman-
Petchel, Dan Citron, George Contant, Mike Dixon, Heather
Hansen, Lee and Linda Jennings, Amy Justice, Clare and Bob
Lawrence, Willis Phelps Jr., Bob Steves, Jennifer and 'Skull Man.'

For sharing expertise about hauntings in Fort Delaware
and providing the HAUR rankings for this volume:
East Coast Society for Paranormal Encounters (ECSPE)
founder Lou DiMieri

For their proofreading and suggestions:
Barbara Burgoon, Marianna Dyal, Sue Moncure,
Ted Stegura and Jacob Marino.

To the Fort Delaware staff, including, but not limited to: the park
administrators, rangers, historians and volunteers, such as Becky,
Keith, Will, George, Dan—as well as Lee and Dale, who had
worked on the tours in the early years—plus the Gift Shop folks,
and Captain Jim Harris and his *Delafort* crew: I appreciate having
had the opportunity to be associated with Fort Delaware for the
last 10 years. It's been a pleasure and an honor to work with
such a fine, talented and pleasant group of folks.

Also available from Myst and Lace Publishers, Inc.

Spirits Between the Bays Series

Volume I
Pulling Back the Curtain
(October 1994)

Volume II
Opening the Door
(March 1995)

Volume III
Welcome Inn
(September 1995)

Volume IV
In the Vestibule
(August 1996)

Volume V
Presence in the Parlor
(April 1997)
Volume VI
Crying in the Kitchen
(April 1998)

Volume VII
Up the Back Stairway
(April 1999)

Volume VIII
Horror in the Hallway
(September 1999)

Volume IX
Phantom in the Bedchamber
(June 2000)

DelMarVa Murder Mystery Series

FIRED!
(May 1998)
Halloween House
(May 1999)

Biography

Matt Zabitka: Sports
(April 2002)

Other Ghost Books

Possessed Possessions
Haunted Antiques, Furniture and
Collectibles
(March 1996)

Possessed Possessions 2
More Haunted Antiques, Furniture
and Collectibles
(September 1998)

Terrifying Tales
of the Beaches and Bays
(March 2001)

Terrifying Tales 2
of the Beaches and Bays
(April 2002)

Ghosts
(August 2001)

Baltimore Ghosts
History, Mystery, Legend and Lore
(August 2004)

Folklore

Stairway over the Brandywine
A Love Story
(February 1995)

Disappearing Delmarva
Portraits of the Peninsula People
(August 1997)

Friends, Neighbors & Folks
Down the Road
(September 2003)

History

Lighthouses of New Jersey
and Delaware
(April 2005)

Treasure Hunting
Seek and You Shall Find
(April 2001)

TABLE OF CONTENTS

Introduction

Let's Take a Step Back in Time

There's something intriguing about Fort Delaware. I guess I can best describe the isolated historic site as being both mysterious and addictive.

My first visit was as a teenager in the early 1960s. And what youngster wouldn't be fascinated by a weekend trip to a Civil War fortress—surrounded by a moat and located on Pea Patch Island? After arriving by a small makeshift ferry boat named the *Miss Kathy*, there was a one-mile walk along a dirt path to an immense Civil War relic that had been pretty much untouched since the federal government deactivated the fort in the 1940s.

A very historic and haunted state park

In 1951, Fort Delaware on Pea Patch Island became one of the First State's earliest state parks, but it wasn't in great shape. The buildings and grounds were in need of repair and attention. But for visiting youngsters, an afternoon exploring the threatening dungeons, running across the parade ground and looking for Yankee and Rebel spirits in decaying structures was an exciting way to spend one's time.

Today, much older and with a different perspective, I return regularly to the granite-walled fortress, but not as a visitor. Instead, I'm fortunate to be part of the cast conducting the evening Ghost/History Lantern Tours, offered during the spring, summer and early fall. It's a role I've been playing since 1997, when Delaware state parks historian Lee Jennings suggested he and I develop the evening guided historic walks—with a heavy dose of hauntings and humor.

Having conducted nearly 100 of these tours has allowed me to see the mighty fortress in a different light, especially when

1

compared to most tourists who visit during daytime hours to enjoy the park's acclaimed living history programs.

As I stop at familiar locations—where fort historians Dan Citron and George Contant and I tell tales and facts to our visitors—I take care to listen carefully to my colleagues. Each time, I learn more about the island's history. I see something new in the brick and granite powder magazines (that also served as confinement areas, sometimes referred to as "dungeons"), and I appreciate our visitors' reports of apparitions, unexplained "sightings," photographic evidence of supposed "spirit energy" and dramatic temperature drops recorded on digital thermometers.

Some believe the potential for spirited sightings on Pea Patch Island is high. About 33,000 Confederate prisoners were housed on the marshy acreage during the Civil War, and the Rebel death toll was close to 2,500. Conditions were dismal, and death to many was a relief. Some passed away by disease, others by suicide, and a fair number died trying to escape from the island.

For many unfortunate souls, both Union and Confederate, their departure was a ride in a wooden box, on a slow moving craft called the "death boat" to a mass grave at Finn's Point, New Jersey. Now a National Cemetery, Yankees and Rebels lie beside one another in hallowed ground.

This view of Fort Delaware was taken from the ferry, Delafort, *which for many years has been captained by Jim Harris.*

On the tour, these stories and others that detail specific ghostly encounters are part of the program. And the question lingers: *Do some of these troubled spirits remain within the Civil War fort's walls?*

From serious historians to amateur ghost hunters, from youngsters of 8 to grandparents in their 80s, there is universal fascination as we cross the drawbridge over the moat, pass beyond the 10-foot-tall, black iron doors and arrive in the dark hall-like entrance (called the sallyport).

Tension fills the damp and dark surroundings as Dan, in a Union officer's uniform, shares the circumstances of the death of Private Stefano. I won't give much away in terms of a surprise ending, but I will say that the visitors' initial nervousness gives way to screams at our first stop. Bumps in the night and unexpected, "unexplained" developments offer a balanced mix of horror and history throughout the two-and-a-half-hour guided excursion.

In nearly a decade of working on this fascinating edu-tainment process I have seen little children cry, grown men turn

The 'dungeons' are a popular attraction, even during daytime visits. Notice the orbs captured in this photograph. Ghost hunters believe these round spots indicate the presence of spirit energy. Similar globes appear on pictures taken at numerous sites throughout the island.

back as they entered the "tunnel-like" passage into the "dungeons" and a young lady argue with her boyfriend, pleading to "go back to Delaware City" rather than proceed on the tour. These, however, are the few extreme cases of fortress jitters. Apparently, the imposing size and sight of the stone castle makes the fainthearted want to head for the hills—or in this case, the safety of the mainland.

The overwhelming reactions during the program are surprise and awe. Surprise in the sense of "What was that?" and awe, as in, "Why haven't I come here before?" and "I never knew there was so much history here, and it's so close to home."

When that occurs, our very distinctive ghost tour mission has reached its mark. You see, the intent was never to deliver an actual ghost, packaged and gift wrapped for delivery. Instead, the tours are a lure, a supernatural bribe to entice folks to visit and experience this historic wonder that Delmarva has at its footstep. Once there for the ghost tour, the setting and stories allow the history to come alive and to amaze even repeat visitors. They learn about the important role the island and its fortress played throughout the nation's history, and many return to see the daytime living history programs offered throughout the week.

The ramparts offer a good view of the interior of the fort.

'Ghost Waters'

In 1999, two years after the tours began, the Discovery Channel sent a film crew to Fort Delaware from Impact Television Productions to produce a segment for the program *Ghost Waters*. The one-hour special premiered on Halloween night, and it is still shown each year during October on various cable channels.

The announcer labels Fort Delaware as "one of the most haunted sites in the United State near the water."

The crew spent three days at the fort, shooting footage and conducting interviews. After marveling at the isolated location, the eerie settings and the wonderful stories, some production personnel admitted they were very uncomfortable while filming in certain secluded sections of the fort.

In my opinion, it is the island—with its lack of electricity, absence of modern intrusions (such as automobile traffic and jeers of passers-by)—that is our ghost tour's greatest asset. This is especially true when comparing the Fort Delaware production to guided walks offered in public and populated locales, such as Williamsburg, Gettysburg, Philadelphia and Cape May.

But not everyone who boards the ferry *Delafort* is a believer. During the orientation at the Delaware City dock, we find out

A moat surrounds the massive fort, which is built of brick and granite.

5

who believe in ghosts, who want to see a ghost, who want to hunt for ghosts and, finally, who have been dragged along and who have no interest in history, the fort or visitors from the other side.

Not surprisingly, these first-time reluctant participants are among those who end up having the best time. And, as the old saying goes, "For those who believe, no explanation is necessary. For those who don't believe, no explanation is satisfactory."

Time for a book

After all these years, helping with the tours, telling the folklore and hearing the history and continued reports of sightings, I decided that the ghosts of Fort Delaware deserved a book of their own.

Over the last few seasons on the island I took a number of photographs at the fort, capturing some of the highlights of the tours. I also began a file about unusual events that were reported in nearby Delaware City and New Castle.

Historian George Contant, right center, shares some history about the fort on Pea Patch Island with visitors prior to boarding the ferry Delafort.

A few tales of phantoms and restless spirits not on the island also are in this book. These, along with a fair number of photographs of locations on Pea Patch Island and in the nearby vicinity, should enhance the stories. There's even a new Legend and Lore piece to tease your imagination and, hopefully, make you wonder "what if?"

An old Irish legend says ghosts cannot cross water. If that's true, then the phantoms on Pea Patch Island are trapped there forever. That's another good reason their stories deserve to be heard.

Until our next book about the unusual and unexplained,

Happy Hauntings,

Ed Okonowicz
In Fair Hill, Maryland,
at the top of the Delmarva Peninsula
Spring 2006

Author's note: Regular readers of our books may find a few of these stories about Fort Delaware repeated from some of our previous volumes. This was done in order to bring all of the stories up to date and to offer a total package of the fort's history and haunts in one volume. However, most of the stories in this book include photographs that illustrate the tales, and in some cases the older stories have been updated with new information. Thank you for your understanding and for reading our books.

Contact Information: The fort, which is a state park, is located on Pea Patch Island in the Delaware River. Access is by boat. The dock is located in Delaware City, several miles south of New Castle, Delaware.

Fort Delaware is open weekends and holidays, the last weekend in April through September. The fort presents the Ghost/History Lantern Tours on certain weekend evenings in the spring, summer and early fall. It also offers special Halloween/Fright-type tours during October.

Admission to the fort is free. There is a charge for the round-trip boat transportation to and from the island. There is a charge for the Ghost Tours and for certain special events. Group tours are available.

To make group arrangements, or for information on operating hours, living history programs and special events and ghost tours, call (302) 834-7941, or visit the web site at www.visitthefort.com/index.html

ECSPE Rates
Fort Delaware's Haunts

When it came time to put together our tombstone rating of this book's haunted sites, it was obvious that I had to talk to Lou DiMieri. The New Castle, Delaware, resident is founder of the East Coast Society for Paranormal Encounters (ECSPE), a group whose members explore haunted sites throughout the region.

ECSPE

"We try to discover explanations or reasons about the unusual things that happen," Lou said.

Armed with a satchel full of electronic and photographic equipment, Lou and his most active members have visited such historic sites as Fort Mifflin, Rockwood Museum and, frequently, Fort Delaware.

Lou estimated that he has been on Pea Patch Island, studying paranormal activity in and outside Fort Delaware on more than two dozen occasions.

"Overall, out of a 1 to 10 rating, with 10 being the most active, I'd give Fort Delaware an 8, with no problem at all," Lou said. "Fort Mifflin, outside Philadelphia, would get a 9. You can't come out of there without something strange happening."

Lou DiMieri while on a guided tour and ghost investigation at Rockwood Museum

Photo provided by Alfred Bestwick

8

And the "something" Lou refers to can be different manifestations depending upon the site. At Fort Mifflin, he explained, electromagnetic energy tends to suck the power out of batteries. At Rockwood Museum, he's gotten reports of smells and a few interesting orbs (round balls of light) in photographs. But at Fort Delaware, sightings of apparitions and a very high number of orbs are commonplace.

"Fort Delaware is a good place to take new members of our organization. It's a good ice-breaking place to get them started," Lou said. He explained that since the groups at the fort are large, his novices are not as uneasy as they would be with a few people in a dark cemetery. He added that there's a good chance that even beginners will get something unusual in their photographs, and they find that reinforcement satisfying.

About the ratings

Several chapters in this book contain a series of tombstones, indicating the site's Haunt and Unexplained Reports rating (HAUR, pronounced "horror").

The HAUR scale represents ECSPE's recommendations based on such factors as frequency of reports, on site investigations, orb count, electronic voice phenomena (EVP), temperature readings, historical events, press and media reports, potential and overall interest in the location.

The level of unexplained activity will range from a low of 1 tombstone (stating the site is merely "active") to a top rating of 5 tombstones (for those locations with "serious hauntings" or having "significant potential"). A place with no haunting history—to ECSPE's present knowledge—or the site of a legend, will not be rated.

Hopefully, those interested in conducting investigations or visiting these public sites will find these ratings helpful.

For information: Lou DiMieri conducts investigations at private homes, museums and other sites upon request. His DVDs—*Chilling Stories and Photos of the Paranormal, Volumes 1 & 2*—are for sale, and feature sights and sounds captured during his investigations. For more information about his organization, DVDs and tours, contact him at (302) 325-9315, at delawareghosthunters@hotmail.com or visit his web site at www.freewebs.com/ecspe

An American flag flies about the historic fort that has overlooked the shipping lanes of the Delaware River for nearly 150 years.

Historical Summary of the Forts on Pea Patch Island

Dr. W. Weir Mitchell, a Philadelphia surgeon who visited the fort in July 1863, when it was most crowded, described the conditions as 'an inferno of detained Rebels.'

In the middle of the Delaware River, east of Delaware City between the opposite shorelines of Delaware and New Jersey, stands Pea Patch Island. And while many have asked questions about the presence of Civil War ghosts within the island's fort, there are others who continue to argue over how the island got its name and when it actually came into existence.

According to the late Delaware journalist, W. Emerson Wilson—in his short book entitled, *Fort Delaware*, published by the University of Delaware Press—Colonial maps did not even indicate that the island existed at that bend in the Delaware River.

Spilling the peas

According to legend, several hundred years ago a wooden ship carrying peas and stones was grounded on a shoal in the middle of the river. Soon the cargo of peas, which had spilled from the wrecked ship, sprouted, took root and formed the beginnings of the island that has since grown to its present size.

In the late 1700s, Major Pierre L'Enfant, who designed the layout of Washington, D.C., recommended that military fortifications be constructed on the island. It was during the War of 1812 that the first defenses were established, and others were built later.

11

The current fort, in the shape of a large pentagon, was completed in 1861. These fortifications, constructed of granite and brick, were built to protect growing cities along the Delaware River, particularly Philadelphia, Wilmington and the New Jersey coastal towns.

But Fort Delaware and its defenders were to see none of the heroic action that provides material for glorious paintings featuring brave soldiers in Civil War battle scenes.

No ships nor enemy troops ever challenged Fort Delaware's defenses. Its 156 cannons were never fired in anger. No enemy flags were captured on its surrounding grounds, no major battles were won or lost, no cavalry charges were signaled by the bugler's call.

Instead, the impressive structure, with its dark, thick walls and 30-foot-wide moat—complete with drawbridge—gained its infamous reputation as nothing more than a deadly, depressing prison camp. Today it stands as Delaware's only tangible link to the War Between the States, or War of Northern Aggression (depending upon your point of view).

Initially, no one thought of using Fort Delaware as a prison. But in the earliest days of the Civil War, decision makers in the U.S. War Department decided that the fort's isolated island location was ideal for use as a prison.

The ferry delivers visitors to a dock that leads to the island. When they reach the end of the dock, a jitney transports them to the fort entrance.

Use as a prison

In April 1862, 258 Confederate prisoners, many from Virginia, became the first of 33,000 Southern soldiers who would eventually be imprisoned on the Delaware River island. Since the fort was not built for use as a prison, the first captives were housed in rooms with little ventilation that had been built as powder magazines to hold ammunition.

These sites eventually became known as the "dungeons." But, as more defeated Rebels arrived, the inside of the fort was overflowing with prisoners, and new facilities were constructed in the marshy wetlands of the island. These wooden shanties provided little heat in the damp winters—the prisoners had one or two stoves for every 200 men—and poor ventilation during the humid, mosquito-infested summers. Eventually, up to 13,000 Confederate prisoners were held captive at one time, during the summer of 1863—immediately following the Battle of Gettysburg.

At that time, historians believe that Fort Delaware was the second largest populated city in the state of Delaware.

Death, however, also set up shop on Pea Patch Island. Poor living conditions and rampant disease are said to be the largest killers of the Rebel captives. Because the health conditions were so deplorable and contributed to the death of so many Rebel prisoners, some historians have referred to Fort Delaware as the "Andersonville of the North," referencing the infamous Georgia prison where Yankee captives died from neglect and disease.

According to some records, approximately 2,500 prisoners died at Fort Delaware. Seven of those were shot, 11 drowned and the rest succumbed to the ravages of sickness and disease.

In a brochure provided to visitors at the fort, entitled *Prison Camp Trail*, Dr. W. Weir Mitchell, a Philadelphia surgeon who visited the fort in July 1863, when it was most crowded, described the conditions as "an inferno of detained Rebels."

Weir said, "A thousand ill; twelve thousand on an island which should hold four; the general level three feet below low water mark; twelve deaths a day from dysentery, and the living having more life on them than in them. Occasional lack of water and, thus, a Christian nation treats the captives of the sword."

Because of the high water table, the dead that were buried on the island began rising from their shallow crypts, being pushed back onto the earth by the pressure of the water. Prison

13

authorities realized that Pea Patch Island could not hold its dead. Some superstitious officials suggested that perhaps even *dead* Rebels were not happy remaining on the island of misery.

Riding the 'Death Boat'

To solve the burial problem, during the Civil War 2,436 deceased Confederate soldiers were transported on the "death boat," to what is now known as Finn's Point National Cemetery in New Jersey. Their names are listed at the base of a tall monument, but they rest in unmarked graves.

Also in the brochure *Prison Camp Trail* there is a statement from the journal of Robert James Coffey, of Company G, 202nd Regiment, Pennsylvania Volunteers. The Yankee soldier wrote, "We took boats over to the New Jersey coast for burial, and sometimes five or six in one day. This . . . was a harder duty for a soldier to face than any fight upon the field or picket line. To have to jump into a boat with five or six men who died of smallpox or other deadly and contagious fevers was a bitter pill to swallow."

Other Rebels, deciding they had nothing to lose—tried to leave the island before they were sealed in a six-foot wooden box. An unknown number—perhaps more than a thousand— escaped or died trying to do so. Some hid in coffins or disguised themselves as Yankee guards. Others made rafts of driftwood, used canteens as floats or stole small boats. And, perhaps the

The entrance to the fort is approached over the moat. Well before the fort was built, Blackbeard the Pirate, a frequent visitor to the area, was said to have buried his treasure on Pea Patch Island.

most desperate, slipped through privy holes and swam toward the river and freedom.

In July 1862, more than 200 prisoners escaped the island in a single night. Their goal was to reach the Delaware shore, connecting with some of the many Southern sympathizers in the First State and then make it back through Maryland into Virginia.

Who knows how many escapees perished in the cold, swift flowing waters of the Delaware River while trying to reach shore? That is one question that will never be answered.

But some believe that many restless spirits, who were unable to return to the familiar soil of their Southern homeland, still roam the coastline of Delaware. On dark, misty nights, men in wet gray uniforms have been seen in the alleyways of Delaware City, along the waterfronts of the coastal towns of New Jersey, in the dungeons of the deserted fort and in the reeds and brush of the Pea Patch Island wetlands. Frustrated, these unsettled specters appear lost and weary from years of seeking the eternal rest that they have never found.

Traveling back in time

When there's not too much tourist activity, particularly in the winter months, stand on the shoreline in Delaware City and look east, out toward Pea Patch Island. The stillness of the passing water and the clear open sky frame a portrait in time of the Civil War-era citadel known as Fort Delaware.

Gaze at the distant gray and red structure of brick and granite in the early morning—when the mist and fog hover over the surface of the river, fighting to survive a few more precious moments before the sun burns them off—and you travel into another dimension . . . where the past still exists.

That view, now in the earliest days of the 21st century, is exactly the same scene as was experienced by Union and Confederate troops when they boarded wooden boats and headed for the island during the Civil War, more than 140 years ago.

In the following chapters of this book, the focus will be on the unexplained incidents, mysterious sightings and photographic puzzles that have been reported by workers and visitors, historians and ghost hunters—demonstrating the close connection between history and hauntings that still exists on and around Pea Patch Island.

15

Contemporary Apparition in the Heronry

Most visitors to Pea Patch Island focus on the fort, the barracks and even the moat. They're the main attractions. Fewer tourists walk into the northern section of the island, known as the heronry or rookery. Maybe there's good reason they stay away.

Several years ago, a local artist spent a considerable amount of time on the island during the off-season, when the fort and island are closed to the public—from October through March.

For this artist, painting wildlife scenes near the nature trails to the north of the fort was her main interest.

After being there several months, she became familiar with the park personnel and got to know many of the staff on a first-name basis.

One afternoon, while painting not far from a pathway, she looked up from her sketchpad and noticed a young boy walking toward her. The youngster was some distance away, and the artist turned back to her work.

As she continued to draw, she thought it was strange that a school-age boy was on the island during the week, on a school day, in the off-season. She looked up from her sketchpad and noticed that the boy was much closer, near enough that she could make out his clothing—a red shirt, tan shorts, dark hair. She estimated that he was about 12 to 14 years old, and she saw that he was soaking wet, as if he had just jumped out of a shower with his clothes on.

Looking down at her painting again, for no more than two seconds, she raised her head and caught a last glimpse of the figure as he slowed faded from view—essentially, disappearing before her eyes.

16

Naturally, the evaporation of the young figure caused a bit of concern and the artist packed up her drawing implements and rushed out of the wooded area, heading toward the fort.

As she crossed over the moat, she saw the park superintendent and mentioned her sighting, noting her concern about the unexplainable sighting of a young boy. Then she added that she was sure it hadn't been a ghost because it wasn't wearing a Confederate or Union uniform.

The park official asked her what the boy was wearing, and she responded with a description of the soaked red and khaki clothing.

Softly, the park superintendent replied, "That sounds like the boy who washed up on the island two days ago. He fell off a boat and drowned, and he was wearing a red shirt and tan shorts."

Apparently, not only Civil War ghosts are roaming Pea Patch Island.

The wooded area at the north end of the island serves as the largest Atlantic Coast heronry north of Florida, hosting species of egrets, herons and ibis. It also was the site of a contemporary haunting, involving the apparition of a young boy.

17

Two stoves provided heat for the more than 200 prisoners housed in each barracks. There were three levels for sleeping in the wooden building, where it was very cold in winter and hot and humid in summer.

Ghosts in the Barracks

When they returned hours later, many of the weekend soldiers found that their equipment had been rummaged through and tossed around. But the new structure had been locked, and no one had been inside.

In the summer of 2001, workers constructed a replica of a Civil War prison barracks on Pea Patch Island. The modern builders used original plans and placed the building where many similar structures had stood during the Civil War.

On the jitney ride from the dock to the fort, the recording stresses that the building is the only accurately constructed Civil War-era, prisoner of war barracks building in the United States.

Some people believe if you make things exactly as they were, the ghosts will come back to stay. Maybe that's what happened the weekend of the dedication of the wooden structure, in mid-August 2001.

Pea Patch Island was much more active than usual during those few days because it was the annual Garrison Weekend, a time set aside for visiting re-enactors—both Union and Confederate—to meet at Fort Delaware. Each year they drilled on the island during the day, adding to the fort's ongoing living history programs. And one of the great attractions to the visiting re-enactors is that they were able to stay overnight on Pea Patch Island.

Usually, solders from the opposing armies camped outside, in tents beside burning campfires, creating a picture perfect Civil War-era image.

19

This particular year, however, the Rebels were going to be accommodated in an even more realistic setting. They were going to spend the night in the newly constructed barracks.

The original 80-foot-long buildings each held between 200-300 prisoners during the Civil War. On this weekend, a small group of men dropped off their belongings in the wooden shelter and planned to return later that evening to sleep overnight.

When they arrived back hours later, several of the weekend soldiers found that their equipment had been rummaged through and tossed around. But the new structure had been locked, and no one had been able to get inside.

During the rest of the weekend, several re-enactors who had slept in the barracks said they felt uneasy. A few reported some of their belongings being lost or moved around. Others said they heard tapping on the roof and under the floor. There was even a claim by one modern-day Rebel prisoner that he saw a canteen float across the barracks.

Since that opening weekend, visitors have asked staff members: "Is the barracks haunted like the fort?"

It's too early to answer for sure.

It takes a while for apparitions and tales to develop and spread by word of mouth. But here's something to consider: The solitary wooden building, set apart from the fort and standing in an open field, represents scores of similar structures that covered

The reconstructed prison barracks on Pea Patch Island is the only such Civil War structure in existence in the country.

about 15 acres of the island during the Civil War.

At one time, many of these buildings held thousands of depressed, injured and diseased prisoners. And they all had one thing in common—none wanted to be stuck on Pea Patch Island.

Perhaps this one rebuilt barracks has become more than its intended purpose, to serve as an example of how many of the captive Rebels lived while they were imprisoned at Fort Delaware.

The barracks, viewed from the fort's ramparts

Maybe the new, carefully reconstructed barracks has become a "ghost magnet." The building may be attracting the restless spirits of those who suffered and died in similar structures while they were prisoners.

The doorway into the fort is an impressive entrance. One Halloween evening, at the end of a ghost tour as visitors were leaving the fort, two of the tourists fell into the moat.

Love at First Sight(ing)

The woman marched out of the sallyport, across the moat walk-way, and sat on a large block of granite to await the arrival of the ferry, Delafort. *'No way am I going back inside that haunted fort,' she said 'It's really haunted!'*

The third year after we had started the Friday evening Ghost/History Lantern Tours at the fort, we guided a group of about 90 visitors across the moat and stopped under the dark brick arches in the sallyport.

The historian had finished presenting the tale of the death of Private Stefano, and I began to share a ghost story.

Suddenly, a young woman in her mid 20s screamed, "HE TOUCHED MY ARM!"

Everyone on the tour, including guides and guests, stopped and turned toward the sound of her shaking voice.

"What did you say?" I asked, speaking loudly enough for my question to echo through the shadowy hall.

"I SAID, 'A CONFEDERATE SOLDIER WALKED RIGHT BY ME, AND HE TOUCHED MY ARM!' " The woman's answer was clear and bold, with no hesitation. She was absolutely sure a spirit from the past had made physical contact with her. And she was not pleased.

As I asked for more details, I could see the crowd close in and try to hear every word of the nervous victim's response. Plus, I calculated that the strange incident would easily generate a few hundred tickets for upcoming ghost tours as soon as word of the encounter spread through the friend-of-a-friend, urban-legend-style, verbal pipeline.

After repeating her brief brush with a ghostly stranger in a gray uniform, the woman announced, "I'm out of here! I want to go home!"

Politely, the state park historian on the tour explained that we were standing on an island, and that the ferry to the mainland would not return for about two-and-a-half hours. The frightened woman wasn't going anywhere beyond the island marsh grass.

At the same time, the woman's escort, who had brought her to Fort Delaware's evening ghost tour on a "first date," impatiently

The darkness of the sallyport, even in daylight, may add to visitors' uneasiness. It is the location of several ghostly sightings.

said that she was holding up
the tour. He also inferred
that she should come along
into the fort and enjoy the
rest of the evening.

A brief exchange of
opinions occurred, and the
woman marched out of the
sallyport, across the moat
walkway, and sat on a large
block of granite to await the
arrival of the ferry, *Delafort.*
"No way am I going back
inside that haunted fort," she
said "It's really haunted!"

*This cistern block in the sallyport is
where a young woman stood when
the Rebel ghost touched her arm.*

Meanwhile, Mister Right moved off in the opposite direction,
meshing into the excited crowd. Apparently, the woman's first-
date escort was eager to experience the remaining portion of the
tour without guilt or distraction from his frightened companion.

With that exciting incident setting the mood, many of the
other folks on the tour admitted they also wanted to be touched
by a Civil War-era visitor from another dimension.

At the conclusion of the night's program, we all expected to
see the victimized young woman, who last had been seen sitting
on the far side of the moat. But she was gone.

We later learned that one of the park rangers saw her seated
alone, and he found out why she had been frightened on the
tour. Rather than have her wait until the arrival of the ferry, he
took her back to the mainland on the park workboat. Then he
bought her a cup of coffee, and he even drove her home, so she
would not have to have another encounter with Mister Right.

The strangest part of the story is that, according to some
island workers, three years later, the frightened woman and the
park ranger—who met as a result of her ghostly encounter—
were married and, to this day, are living happily ever after.

Accidental Death
of Private Stefano

Because of the pressing demand for troops, the Civil War provided immigrants to the U.S. with jobs and opportunities to learn a trade and master the English language. One such young man, who had hoped to benefit from the war, was Private Stefano. He was an Italian who joined the Union army and, eventually, was assigned to Fort Delaware. On the island, he acted as an aide to several Confederate generals, who had been captured and imprisoned within the fort.

To maintain security and control over these Confederate officers, they were separated from their enlisted men, who lived in wooden barracks constructed across the island, outside the walls

The slippery stairs where Private Stefano fell and died

of the stone fort. The captured officers, however, were housed in a series of rooms located directly above the sallyport entrance.

Stefano's job was to work as an aide or assistant to the Rebel officers, running errands and securing items they requested.

Thinking he would be viewed favorably, and possibly even promoted, if he did his job well, the young Italian, who spoke very little English, was often seen running about the fort.

Because of the region's high humidity, the dark granite steps leading from the sallyport to the upper level officers' rooms were often coated with a slick layer of moisture. Even today, the stairs are very slippery during rainy weather, and also can be treacherous during the dry season.

Repeatedly, Stefano's fellow soldiers told him to "slow down" and "be careful on the stairs." The Italian's response usually was a stream of foreign muttering in his

Another view of Stefano's stairs, one of the first stops on the Ghost/History tours

native tongue that those within earshot could not understand. However, they guessed Stefano's responses could be anything from a simple "Thank you," to a rude "Mind your own business."

Unfortunately, the eccentric private's muttered messages will never be known, since he was the victim of an unfortunate accident that some witnesses believed was the result of his own stubbornness.

One day, while racing down the slippery stairs, Stefano lost his balance and tumbled, landing head-first at the base of the south stairwell. Since granite is much harder than bone, Stefano's skull had been cracked open like a coconut, and his blood seeped onto the stone floor.

Even today, workers and visitors point out locations where they claim to have seen remnants of the dead private's blood, very close to the spot where the young soldier died.

The room above the sallyport, from which a re-enactor who worked at the fort, saw an apparition of a Confederate soldier

Ghosts (or Re-enactors) Above the Sallyport?

Re-enactors at historic sites occasionally are mistaken for ghostly visitors, and unexplained spirited visitors have been mistaken for humans.

An important fact that will be mentioned often in this book is: Re-enactors often show up without warning. This fact of life at Civil War sites has a significant bearing on the authenticity of ghostly sightings.

One Friday evening, as we were waiting to board the ferry *Delafort*, I pointed toward 13 people standing on the dock that were dressed in Confederate-style attire. I asked the historian, "How many people are working tonight?"

"Just you and me," he replied.

When I asked for an explanation about the Rebel-clad group, he explained, "They're re-enactors. They're going to a Civil War fort, so they get dressed up in their period costumes. They can't wear them to church or work, so they put them on when they come here. It happens from time to time. It's not really that unusual."

Later, during a trip to Gettysburg, I noticed a gentlemen dressed like General Lee pumping gas at a convenience store in the middle of town, while a Union general walked by drinking a cup of coffee. (There seem to be a lot of high-ranking re-enactors. I guess if you had a choice, why not decide to promote yourself to walk around as a general rather than as a private?)

At the Farnsworth House dining room one evening, my wife and I—who were dressed in semi-formal, 20th-century civilian attire—were outnumbered by the other diners, including women clad in floor length dresses and bonnets, officers in dress uniforms and civilians in frock coats and top hats.

Based on those few experiences, I realized that re-enactors at historic sites occasionally are mistaken for ghostly visitors, and unexplained spirited visitors have been mistaken for humans.

During the early years of the ghost tours, we were able to lead visitors upstairs, into the rooms directly above the sallyport. In those rooms, the high-ranking Confederate officers were housed, separated from the masses of lower-ranking soldiers who occupied the wooden barracks.

An unusual incident occurred to an excellent and experienced re-enactor named Bob Steves, who was involved with the Ghost/History Tours for many years.

One day, Bob arrived to work at the fort, walked up to the second floor—where the Rebel officers had lived—and entered a room that was used as a dressing area.

· While he was putting on his uniform, Bob noticed another re-enactor, who apparently had arrived earlier and was already dressed. The stranger walked by Bob's doorway and headed down the narrow hall.

Instinctively, Bob called out a greeting and went

Haunted hallway above the sallyport

into the hall. He planned to talk to the person with whom he assumed he would be working during the day.

The hallway was empty. There was no one there.

But what was even stranger is that the hallway stops at a dead end. There is no way the mysterious walker could have returned without passing by or through Bob.

After the incident, Bob checked the grounds and buildings, but there was no other re-enactor on the island at that time. He talked to the workmen, who confirmed that no one had accompanied them over earlier in the day on the workboat.

Bob was the first historical staff member on the island that day. Some suggest the apparition he saw may have been one of Pea Patch Island's very quiet and shy full-time residents.

During the filming of *Ghost Waters*, an interviewer asked Bob his opinion of reports of paranormal activity at Fort Delaware. His response was one of the best I have ever heard.

"Do I think this fort is *haunted?*" Bob replied, repeating the question. Then Bob answered, "If your definition of *haunted* means that it's inhabited by something we can't see in a conventional manner. Yes!"

Rooms above the sallyport served as quarters for many of the higher ranking captured officers.

An apparition appeared to come out of this door, which is not a room, only a narrow closet.

Mystery of the Missing Mess Hall Mantel

There was no doubt on the part of many who worked at Fort Delaware that weekend that some of those in attendance had seen a ghost.

Several special Halloween Ghost Tours were added to Fort Delaware's schedule a year after the Ghost/History Lantern Tours began. These excursions were a bit different from the summer and early fall presentations, adding some drama, special effects and jump-out fright for the audiences' enjoyment.

Today, the number of weekend, Halloween-theme tours on the island has been expanded greatly and they offer a "fright night" approach with a menu of special effects—including eerie lighting and smoke-filled rooms. For those few weekends in October, history takes a back seat to horror.

'Quoth the Raven'

In the early ghost tour years, things were a bit more tame. I did a vampire theme presentation and the historian offered a reading of Edgar Allan Poe's masterpiece, "The Raven." It was on the last weekend in October, on Halloween night as I recall, when a "classic" haunting occurred on Pea Patch Island.

Dale Fetzer, a park historian at the time and a very talented actor and re-enactor, was scheduled to read "The Raven." Attired in a frock coat, top hat and white shirt, Dale entered the room and took his place at the far, dimly lit corner of the Mess Hall.

A small candle in a metal holder was his only prop. It flickered beside the leather bound volume of Poe's poetic handiwork.

Dale welcomed the visitors, paused behind the raised, upright, standing desk, and began to read the words, first published in 1845, not too long before the start of the Civil War.

> Once upon a midnight dreary,
> while I pondered weak and weary,
> Over many a quaint and curious volume
> of forgotten lore,
> While I nodded, nearly napping,
> suddenly there came a tapping,
> As of some one gently rapping,
> rapping at my chamber door.
> 'Tis some visitor,' I muttered,
> 'tapping at my chamber door—
> Only this, and nothing more.'

> Ah, distinctly I remember
> it was in the bleak December,
> And each separate dying ember
> wrought its ghost upon the floor.
> Eagerly I wished the morrow;
> vainly I had sought to borrow
> From my books surcease of sorrow
> sorrow for the lost Lenore
> For the rare and radiant maiden
> whom the angels named Lenore
> Nameless here for evermore.

The room was hushed. The atmosphere intense.

As if the words of the eerie poem had the ability to attract the spirits from the past, some visitors later said they thought that a sudden chill filled the historic room.

No doubt, many in the audience believed that the program's content and dated entertainment style, from an earlier era, was familiar to any spirits that might be lingering from the past.

> Much I marvelled this ungainly fowl
> to hear discourse so plainly,
> Though its answer little meaning
> little relevancy bore;

For we cannot help agreeing
that no living human being
Ever yet was blessed with seeing
bird above his chamber door
Bird or beast above the sculptured bust
above his chamber door,
With such name as 'Nevermore.'

As those in the audience listened intently, and their eyes adjusted to the low glow from the two small lights hanging from the ceiling, several people let out a sudden scream.

They had reacted instinctively to the enveloping darkness that consumed the room when the generator, which powered the lighting, apparently had failed.

Ever the theatrical trooper, Dale calmed the crowd, lifted his candle holder and, by the flickering uneven candlelight, effortlessly completed his reading of "The Raven."

Be that word our sign of parting,
bird or fiend!' I shrieked upstarting—
Get thee back into the tempest
and the Night's Plutonian shore!
Leave no black plume as a token
of that lie thy soul hath spoken!
Leave my loneliness unbroken!
quit the bust above my door!
Take thy beak from out my heart,
and take thy form from off my door!'
Quoth the raven, 'Nevermore.'

And the raven, never flitting,
still is sitting, still is sitting
On the pallid bust of Pallas
just above my chamber door;
And his eyes have all the seeming
of a demon's that is dreaming,
And the lamp-light o'er him streaming
throws his shadow on the floor;
And my soul from out that shadow
that lies floating on the floor
Shall be lifted—nevermore!

When the applause ceased, a satisfied, but slightly mystified, group left the Mess Hall, continued its walk through the Parade Ground and wound its way through the dark and echoing dungeons. The tour ended, and the group of evening visitors passed over the moat and headed to the mainland, leaving Poe's images, the flickering lights and any lingering spirits behind.

But this is where the ghost tale associated with Dale's poetic performance begins.

Mysterious mantel

As expected, some of the cast and crew who had worked on the weekend programs joked about the unexplained lighting problem in the "haunted" Mess Hall. They also mentioned how smoothly Dale had handled the unexpected mini-crisis.

A few of the Fort Delaware staff even suggested, although jokingly, that maybe "the ghosts had played a role in the show" or "offered their own eerie entertainment" to scare both the visitors and the performers.

The rest of the story developed a week later, when Dale ran into a few members of the Fort Delaware Society who had attended his Poe reading. As they got into their conversation about the previous weekend tours, the couple remarked that they found one aspect of Dale's program particularly entertaining.

The room from which the mysterious cleaning lady appeared on Halloween night is really a narrow closet.

36

When he asked for specifics, they said it was when the lady, in the 1860s-style clothing, came out from the room to Dale's left, dusted the mantel and then went back into the room and disappeared.

The visitors said to Dale, "You acted as if you hadn't seen her. In fact, you were so unaware of her presence we were sure she was part of the act."

Anything but.

He did not see the woman, he explained, because there was "NO woman" at the fort who was part of that performance.

Rather than accept his explanation, the couple insisted they had seen a woman dusting the mantel. In fact, they added, the couple who they were with that night also saw the mysterious cleaning woman. There was clear in their mind that someone or something, indeed, had appeared during the performance.

There also was no doubt on the part of some who worked at Fort Delaware that weekend that some of those in attendance had seen a ghost.

In fact, while being interviewed about the incident for the TV program *Ghost Waters*, Dale said, "It was a massive haunting, and I have to tell you it put the hair on the back of my neck up."

But the eerie story took another psychic twist when the fort's staff investigated the so-called "room" from which the cleaning lady was seen entering the Mess Hall.

It's only about 8 inches deep, not even the depth of a child's closet. There is no way a woman, or anyone else, could have been inside that small opening and entered the room.

This troublesome mantel (at right) had been displayed in the Mess Hall. Some believe the object was 'too active,' and both mantels have been removed and hidden from public view.

Also, the entire story involves an object that, some believe, had previously been involved in a paranormal association with Fort Delaware.

A *mantel.*

A mantel that is no longer found in the room. Instead the area above the Mess Hall fireplace has no flat wooden piece upon which to place items for display. The mysterious shelf has been removed, possibly even hidden somewhere—perhaps, so that the public would not be able to examine it. But indications are that a mantel had, at one time, been there—by the marks that remain, exactly where the two removed brackets once were affixed to the wall.

If you look closely in the Mess Hall, there are two vertical marks, above and on either side of the hearth, where the pair of metal brackets held the haunted mantel.

They also have been removed.

"Put into storage," fort officials say, "because the items are not historically accurate. They are not from the proper, historical Civil War era that Fort Delaware is charged with representing."

Some, however, believe the often repeated legend: That the brackets and mantel are held below the fort, in one of several empty water cisterns that has long ago leaked dry. These

The Mess Hall wall as it appears today, without the mantel. Note the two bracket marks, above the hearth, which sources report have been repeatedly painted over, but which continue to reappear.

active or agitated antiques are stored, along with a number of other haunted objects, where they can remain hidden, out of reach and out of sight.

The official story is that an unspecified state parks storage facility does, indeed, "house a considerable number" of older objects, but none are haunted. They're just there, waiting to be used at the proper location—and they will be displayed at the appropriate time.

And what about those vertical marks where the brackets once held the pesky mantel?

Conspiracy theorists and ghost hunters claim they've been told that workmen keep painting over the marks, only to discover that they reappear a few days later—maybe trying to leave a clue that there's more to the sanitized site than meets the average tourist's eye.

"Not true!" state parks personnel protest. They're just waiting for the right mix of concrete, sand and lime to match Civil War-era construction methods. Then they'll patch up the bracket marks and paint them over to match the restored portions of the wall.

"There's no haunted mantel. No conspiracy. No reappearing bracket marks. No cleaning lady apparition. No ghosts!" the state park officials stress.

Perhaps they protest too much.

The kitchen, where re-enactors and seasonal employees cook and work, recreating the food and customs of the Civil War

The Kitchen Ghost
or Fort Delaware's
'Lady in Black'

*The ghost . . . looked around, opened up pots . . . made some
approving sorts of nodding and smiling, and then turned around
and walked into a wall. And that's when everybody got the clue
that this was not just part of the cast.*

—Lee Jennings

Lots of people say they "see ghosts." After many years of
interviewing informants who have made this claim, I have
tried to sort out the credible from the incredible, or the
questionable. Later, during more intense discussion, some of
these folks will admit they "think" they saw a ghost.

Other say they really had "wanted" to see a ghost and that
the eerie shadow in the corner of the old building "just had to
be" a visitor from "the other side."

Then there are the folks I call "ghosters," the paranormal
investigators who visit graveyards, explore old houses and carry
lots of fancy, high-tech equipment. They will spend hours,
patiently waiting in the dark, hoping for that moment when they
can "capture the creature on film" or take that "breakthrough
photograph" that will get them on TV and generate invitations to
present lectures on the ghost conference speakers circuit.

Eventually, anyone listening to reports from many different
sources starts to categorize them according to their credibility.

A police officer offering a first-hand unexplained experience
while he was on duty is certainly higher on the believability list

41

than the elderly lady with poor eyesight, who awakens in the middle of the night and later says she "thinks" she saw a glow coming from the foot of her bed.

It's natural to rate the sources and, more importantly, it is very necessary.

After hearing plenty of reports of "footsteps upstairs" or "bumps in the night in the attic" and even "moving lights in the upstairs window," when a top-level, credible source comes forward, it makes an investigator or writer pause and think: *There really is something to this paranormal business,* and immediately take careful notes to get the story on paper.

This is one of those stories, which I first heard in 1995, and immediately recorded and shared. But it was an incident 10 years later, in 2005, that caused many who saw the evidence, to think there is more to this particular ghost story than hearsay and folklore.

Ghostly sighting

While speaking to Delaware state parks historian Lee Jennings and his wife, Linda, Lee said he had never seen a ghost at the fort, even though he had worked there for several years.

He admitted that while working at the state park on Pea

Heather Hansen, working near the stove in the Officers' Kitchen

Patch Island he had heard footsteps and experienced uneasy feelings.

"It's hard when you're walking in a dark place by yourself," Lee explained, "to not be disconcerted by the sound of somebody behind you that you can't see. I have heard footsteps, I've heard hushed conversations, but most of the time it's just this presence here. It's like you're being followed."

But, he added, his wife said she had seen a ghost at Fort Delaware.

Casually, Linda Jennings said she had witnessed an unexplained event at the fort, and she said paranormal experiences don't bother her. When she was young, walking through cemeteries and reading tombstones was as normal as a day at the mall.

Linda explained that several years ago she had been presenting living history sessions in the fort's kitchen area. On these occasions, she and several other women and their children were dressed in Civil War-era clothing and prepared food in the manner of the period.

It was in the back kitchen, behind the officers' quarters, where she saw the ghost.

"I looked over in the corner," Linda said, "and I saw a lady staring at us. I did a double take and kind of nodded. Because there were children with me, I didn't say anything."

Linda described the stranger as a black

Heather Hansen stands in the corner, near the cold spot, which some believe serves as a portal for visiting spirits. There also have been reports of strange incidents happening in the closet to her left.

woman, about 35 years old and 5'6" tall. She had a scar on her left cheek and wore a blue-and-white, checkered dress with a white collar.

"Her apron was filthy, cruddy," Linda said. "It was singed at the bottom, probably from working in the kitchen. She was there for about an hour. She walked around, came close and examined what we were cooking. She was looking in the pots. She vanished for a short time and then came back. She looked at me. I felt she was nodding approval at what we were doing."

Lee said that during the Civil War there were quite a few free blacks that were employed as help in the fort's kitchens and laundry, both in and outside the fortress structure. Having a black cook present would have been normal in the Union officers' quarters.

"I wanted to try to talk to her," Linda said. "But I didn't get the opportunity. The kids were here cutting carrots and potatoes and onions, and I didn't want to do anything in front of them."

Linda had the impression that at first the Civil War phantom was wondering what was taking place. Then, after the tours of visitors passed through, the ghost realized that the volunteers were re-enacting the past, offering a presentation of what things were like during the Civil War at the fort.

Is such a sighting possible?

"I'm an historian," said Lee. "I know my wife is sensitive to these types of activities more than I am. I believe, and I attach importance to what she says. We have some payroll records of those who worked at the fort. I'd like to see what we can find."

Is it possible that the spirit was responding to the setting and portrayals of the past?

Could it be that accurate representations of the long passed era—with Civil War uniforms, food and equipment—may cause resident ghosts or trapped spirits to be more comfortable and encourage them to appear?

"I think they are here because we are here," said Linda. "They can be there all the time, and we just don't see them."

"Maybe the familiar surroundings help," added Lee. "I recall when we started our work there, walking through the dungeon areas was unpleasant. It was not a nice place to be. You would start out walking, and you end up running to get out.

"But the further we got into the living history program, some of those feelings started to go away. A lot of the uneasiness seemed to disappear. Things seemed to calm down a lot. We had a feeling we had their approval, that we were telling the story and we were telling it right."

Ten years later

As the Fort Delaware ghost tours progressed, more information was developed about the "Ghost in the Kitchen." After hearing about Linda's encounter, ghost hunters, psychics and spiritualists visited the room. They stated that a "cold spot" was present in a corner, on the same side of the room as the stove.

This frigid area is the spot where Linda Jennings had seen the ghostly apparition. On the 1999 television program *Ghost Waters*, Lee described the sighting. "The ghost . . . looked around, opened up pots . . . made some approving sorts of nodding and smiling, and then turned around and walked into a wall. And that's when everybody got the clue that this was not just part of the cast."

As we present the Fort Delaware Ghost/History Lantern Tours, one of the evening's highlights is sharing the story about this unidentified, unexplained visitor in the very room where she had appeared.

On certain tours, ghost hunters have announced that the "ghostly" corner of the room is, in fact, considerably colder than the surrounding area. Lou DiMieri is president of the East Coast Society of Paranormal Encounters (ECSPE), a Delaware-based, ghost hunting group. During his visits, Lou has taken photographs throughout the fort, often capturing orbs (small hazy globes) among the images of buildings and furniture. While in the kitchen, he has measured the "cold" spot with a temperature gauge, which indicated at times the corner is 14 degrees colder than the rest of the room.

Some children and adults have been afraid to walk near the chilly location, while others have rushed to see if they can sense the chill and experience a touch of the passageway or "portal to the other side."

Then on Sept. 9, 2005, something very strange happened.

The ghostly cook made a return visit, but apparently no one had seen her. However, the apparition's presence was captured on a digital camera.

This picture of the Kitchen Ghost was captured by Amy Justice, on her digital camera, while there was no figure visible in the room, during the evening Ghost/History Lantern Tour on Sept. 9, 2005.

Amy Justice, a Bear, Delaware, resident was present on the evening Ghost/History Tour. Soon after the conclusion of the program in the kitchen, small crowds began to cluster around her as she held out her digital camera to display the image of a mysterious figure she had just captured.

Surrounded by a reddish background, in the very corner that has been designated for years as the fort's "cold spot," the dark figure—of a woman wearing a long black dress or flowing gown, with an apron—is the epitome of a ghostly image.

Thanks to Amy, her picture is reproduced in this book, and it remains one of the best paranormal images taken at Fort Delaware.

Did the visitor from the past just happen to pass through the portal from the other side as Amy pressed the button on her camera?

Perhaps.

But maybe there's a better explanation, and one that Linda Jennings had suggested in an interview several years earlier: "They can be there all the time, and we just don't see them."

Capturing the Apparition in the Kitchen

I have had a few people look at the picture, and they will say, 'What am I seeing?' My standard reply is, 'A ghost.'
—Amy Justice

Amy Justice, a minister of the Wiccan faith, lives near Newark, Delaware. Many believe her "Lady in Black" apparition photograph, taken in the Fort Delaware kitchen, is one of the best ghostly images captured at the island prison.

Admitting she was surprised and astonished when she saw the image in her digital camera, Amy added that she had not seen anything in the viewer when she pressed the button to activate the camera.

"I did not see the figure in the viewer as it appeared," Amy said, recalling the September 2005 incident. "What happened was, I had felt the hairs on my neck stand up, and a presence in the room. So I looked over into the 'cold spot' and thought I caught a glimmer of movement. I snapped the picture expecting to possibly see an orb or two, not the apparition that appeared."

Further explaining her surprising discovery, Amy said, "Here we were in a room with tan walls, and no one in front of me, and I had gotten a picture—not only of a woman's figure, but also that the walls had turned red in the picture! This woman matched what I had pictured in my mind when hearing the story about the women gathered for a Civil War cooking re-enactment who had seen the ghost."

Amy was not the only one that evening who reacted with interest and surprise upon seeing her photograph.

"I had more than one person tell me that they went on this tour because they were skeptical that ghosts did exist," Amy said, "and they wanted to know the truth. And that seeing that picture, and knowing that I had no time or way to doctor it from inside the camera, and knowing they had been in the room with me, that ghosts had to be real."

Amy Justice

When asked if she believes in ghosts, Amy, a member of the Delaware Association of Paranormal Investigators, replied, "I certainly do and always have."

Her photograph of the kitchen apparition has been the talk of the paranormal community, and nearly everyone who has seen it has been impressed and has offered an immediate reaction.

"I have had a few people look at the picture," Amy recalled, "and they will say, 'What am I seeing?' My standard reply is, 'A ghost.' "

Few visitors realize that this kitchen doorway is the entrance into the most haunted room in Fort Delaware.

More Unusual Events in the Haunted Kitchen

He [TV cameraman] was so shaken that several years later he convinced his producer to return to the fort to shoot sequences for the Addams Family Marathon, for that Halloween.

—George Contant

few days after Amy Justice sent me the digital image of the "Lady in Black" taken in the haunted kitchen, I sent a copy to fort historic site manager George Contant.

Over the years George has gathered a small collection of letters and images—all related to eerie sightings or unexplained sounds and events—that Pea Patch Island visitors have experienced.

After receiving the picture of the "Lady in Black" in the kitchen, he knew it had been sent to me a week after the tour. But he also assumed that something that good certainly had to have been created or manipulated. After all, there was no way that a picture of an apparition would turn out that well, and certainly not in the very spot that we had pointed out on the tours.

Without a doubt, George told me, he was convinced the photograph was a fake. In fact, he and his son, Jonathan, had created one almost identical to it on their computer, just to see if it could be done.

While standing at the dock in Delaware City, I listened to George's assumptions and then, very clearly, told him that I was sure the image of the "Lady in Black" was captured in the room. I stressed that I had seen the picture immediately after it was

51

taken. There was no way it could have been "doctored" or was manufactured.

Obviously startled, George said he was bothered by the news, since there had been a number of other incidents reported in that corner of the kitchen, which also is the location of a pantry. He talked about the day a film crew from the television station, *Philly 57*, toured the fort and shot several scenes inside the kitchen.

The cameraman, George said, told the rest of his group he wanted to take more footage in the kitchen, so he remained there alone after his colleagues continued exploring the fort.

"While he was in the pantry," George said, "the guy said something smacked him on the back of his shoulder and then it said his name, and the words, 'Get out!' He was so shaken that several years later he convinced his producer to return to the fort to shoot sequences for the Addams Family Marathon, for that Halloween."

That was only one story.

"Last year," George said, "my daughter, Krystin, was a volunteer, working in the laundry. I asked her to go into the pantry and get a pitcher for the enlisted men's Mess Hall. She told me she went into the pantry and, as she started to leave, a voice of an older or mature woman said, 'That's not nice.' Krystin came flying back and told me what had happened."

Other workers and volunteers who've been in the pantry, which is adjacent to the "cold spot," have said they've heard sounds in there.

Heather Hansen, a senior in art conservation and art history at the University of

The closet, which is the door to the left, has been reported as the source of significant paranormal activity.

Delaware, worked as a volunteer and employee at the fort for seven years. She said she has spent a lot of time in the kitchen area and inside the pantry.

Heather explained the cooler temperature in the kitchen is because of the cisterns, which are filled with thousands of gallons of water, and located below that section of the fort. This helps preserve food longer. But while she knows the cisterns caused lower temperatures, she said, "I can't help wondering if there's another reason, sometimes."

One of Heather's jobs was to wait inside the dark closet for the arrival of the ghost tours, and "appear" at the appropriate time.

"The pantry is completely pitch black," she said, "so I tended to wait until right before the group came in to hide. Sometimes I think the interpreters got more frightened on the tours than the visitors did. I didn't mind sitting in the dark, as long as I could hear the stories on the other side of the door. Otherwise, my imagination would get the best of me, wondering if there might be someone in the pantry with me, or if the kitchen ghost was on the other side of the door and I was missing my chance to see her."

While Heather said she's never seen anything resembling a ghost, she has heard her share of stories. "I haven't seen any ghosts myself, but I know that some of the other interpreters have. The people at the fort are like family to me, and they don't have any reason to lie about stories like that. And just because I haven't seen anything yet, doesn't mean I may not in the future."

"Some workers think they hear buzzing," while in the pantry, George said. "Others say they can hear scratching around the walls. But that's just not possible. Those are double brick walls."

Perplexed, George shook his head, ending the conversation. I got the impression that the historian didn't want to talk any longer about the haunted kitchen and its unexplained events—especially since, initially, he thought he had solved the riddle of the unusual and troubling photograph.

I also noticed that after our conversation, George never entered the haunted kitchen during any of the subsequent tours that season. He always remained out in the hall, a safe distance from the "cold spot."

Heather Hansen

Prisoners would hide empty canteens, which they used as life preservers, in the marsh grass outside the walls of the fort. The canteens would help them swim across the river to safety in Delaware City.

Escaping from the Island

Stories persist of hidden 'extra cargo,' in the form of desperate prisoners, who were willing to share a ride inside a coffin with a dead soldier.

Leaving Pea Patch Island was constantly on the minds of both Union and Confederate soldiers. Although the Yankees guarded the Rebel prisoners, the boys in blue had to suffer the same heat and cold and threats of disease as their captives.

With lots of time on their hands, the prisoners spent quite a bit of it trying to think up ways to escape. It's not surprising they came up with a variety of basic and not so obvious methods.

Swimming to safety

Swimming was a simple and obvious option, until the swift current carried hopeful escapees down river and away from the safety of the Delaware shore. A number of swimming Rebels, who were not in the best physical condition, died using this method.

Using flotation devices, or homemade life preservers, proved to work for a while. One of the easiest to come by was a common piece of military equipment that worked well—the canteen. Made of wood at the time, a group of four or more empty canteens were ideal for increasing the swimming escapee's chances of success.

When the Yankees discovered their Rebel guests were using canteens to escape, the Union troops confiscated thousands of hidden canteens from the Rebel barracks—and destroyed them by burning.

There are some reports that Yankees found canteens stashed in the island marsh, obviously hidden for use in an upcoming getaway. Some playful guards left these canteens in place, waiting for the escaping Rebels, but only after the guards had punched holes in the small wooden casks.

Those prisoners who made it to the island shore and wrapped these damaged canteens around their bodies had no idea that their chances of making it to the mainland had been reduced significantly.

On the 'Death Boat'

One ride that the prisoners tried to avoid was a one-way trip off the island in the "Death Boat." This barge carried wooden coffins of prisoners who had died on Pea Patch. The craft of death delivered its lifeless cargo to Finn's Point, New Jersey, a small site north of Fort Mott. At this National Cemetery monuments now mark the two areas where Yankee and Rebel soldiers are buried in mass graves.

Stories persist of hidden "extra cargo," in the form of desperate prisoners who were willing to share a ride inside a coffin with a dead soldier. When the wooden body boxes were delivered to Finn's Point for burial, the escaping Rebel planned to push up the lid and try to run into the woods without attracting the attention of the Yankee guards.

However, one legend is that some escaping prisoners were unable to get out of the coffins. They died, buried alive, while screaming for help and clawing at the inside wooden lid, beside the corpse that made its final ride from the island.

These missing prisoners were never found, and their names were never placed on the plaque, at the base of the Confederate monument, that lists those resting in the mass grave.

Civil War headstones, like this one belonging to a Delaware soldier, are found in cemeteries throughout Delmarva.

Heading for Delaware City

When Confederates were able to escape, they headed west, toward Delaware City, because First State soil offered the best hope for a safer journey back to the South.

The state of Delaware was truly a Border State. Its citizens had mixed feelings about the Civil War, about President Abraham Lincoln and about states rights and slavery. Actually, the entire Delmarva Peninsula, with its 14 counties, has been described accurately as a geographic region where America's North meets South.

Therefore, slave owners and abolitionists were in constant contact, living and working in the same communities, and some were even members of the same family.

A secret underground railroad system to assist members of the Confederate Secret Service and also escaping prisoners operated throughout the peninsula. It consisted of safe houses, transportation networks and supply lines. For political prisoners and Rebel soldiers who were able to get off Pea Patch Island, several routes from Delaware City led toward the South.

Prisoners swam toward the Delaware City coastline, and then would seek help from Confederate sympathizers in the town. Some escapees died and are believed to be buried near some of the old homes in the area, which are said to be haunted.

This river town was an important depot on the escape route and a logical place for a hub that would feed and clothe escaping Rebels. Eventually, they would be smuggled—some in the bottoms of wagons, and others in small fishing boats—toward Smyrna. Other sympathizers were waiting in Dover, then the escapees were moved to Seaford and finally west, onto blockade running boats waiting in the Nanticoke River.

From there, the human cargo was taken to Virginia, where the free prisoners would rejoin their units or enter new ones and head out again to fight the invading Yankees.

There were times, however, when sick prisoners too weak to make the journey home, were cared for by Rebel sympathizers in Delaware City. A number of these escapees died in the cellars and secret rooms of these homes on the mainland, many within sight of the fort. Disposing of the bodies was not easy.

Dead Rebels were held until a funeral occurred. Then they were hidden in the coffin beneath the corpse. Others were buried in the woods or open areas behind homes and some were tossed into the river. There even are stories that dead prisoners were buried in the cellars of the homes where they died.

Perhaps these troubled souls, who never were able to complete their journey home, are unhappy in unmarked sites in Northern soil. This may be the reason that owners of a few old homes in the Delaware watertowns near the fort, have reported paranormal incidents.

One of the original burial sites on Pea Patch Island is believed to be near the brick building on the New Jersey side of the island.

The area near the corner of this fence in the town cemetery is said to contain the unmarked grave of six Confederate soldiers.

A number of Civil War Union veterans are buried in the graveyard surrounding First Presbyterian Church at Second and Jefferson streets.

This area—extending from Second to Williams streets and from Jefferson to Madison streets—serves as a multi-denominational cemetery, divided into separate sections with the remains of citizens from several faiths.

While the Union soldiers each are marked with a distinctive stone, listing their name and unit, it's believed about a half-dozen Confederate soldiers rest in an unmarked grave in the Presbyterian Church section of the block.

According to Fort Delaware historic site manager George Contant, there is a significant area located along the Jefferson Street side of the burial ground, beside the metal fence and in the corner next to the flagpole. In this unmarked plot, where there are no stone or metal grave markers, rest the remains of several Rebel soldiers who died while imprisoned at Fort Delaware.

The Confederate Monument at Finn's Point National Cemetery, near Fort Mott State Park in New Jersey, marks the final resting place for more than 2,400 veterans from the South who died at Fort Delaware.

Finn's Point
National Cemetery

At the north end stands an impressive monument, 85-feet tall and built of white Pennsylvania granite. It was erected in 1910 by the U.S. government to recognize the 2,436 Rebels who were buried in New Jersey's Yankee soil.

A two-lane road off New Jersey Route 49 heads west toward the Delaware River and Fort Mott. Entering the state park, one's attention is drawn to a series of well-preserved, concrete coastal fortifications standing at the river's edge. Tourists climb the metal stairs that lead to the ramparts and observation houses above. Standing there, looking out over the Delaware River, one views the same land and seascape that was seen by U.S. Army defenders during the Spanish-American War and World War I.

From Fort Mott, the east side of Fort Delaware is clearly visible. The ancient, granite pentagon stands close to the edge of the New Jersey side of Pea Patch Island.

Originally designed to defend the Delaware River in the post-Civil War era, construction of the Fort Mott coastal artillery defenses started in 1872. The initial phase, with two gun emplacements, was completed in 1876. The site was expanded in 1896 and the number of gun emplacements was increased.

When completed, the 10- and 12-inch guns at Fort Mott had an effective range of approximately eight miles. At the time, that was a longer range than any of the naval vessels had that might have been involved in an attack. Two tall, iron control towers, still located on the state park grounds, were used to direct and adjust the shellfire upon the enemy.

Combined with the firepower at Fort Delaware on Pea Patch Island and from Fort DuPont, located just south of Delaware City, the three-fort defense of the Delaware River was considered formidable.

However, sometime after World War I, construction of more advanced defenses occurred at Fort Salisbury, near Milford, and at Fort Miles, near Cape Henlopen, both in Delaware, and at Cape May in New Jersey. These defense improvements made the three upriver sites obsolete as defense installations.

As time passed the federal government abandoned Fort Mott. In 1947, the state of New Jersey took it over and opened it to the public in 1951.

Finn's Point National Cemetery is an extremely isolated plot of land, less than a half-dozen acres in size. It's well off the beaten track, with a narrow road leading to and from its iron-gated entrance. It seems like it was hidden intentionally, behind mounds topped by tall swaying marsh grass and a low, well-kept granite wall that encircles the irregular-shaped plot of hallowed ground.

It is the resting place of Fort Delaware's Confederate and Union soldiers, as well as military personnel from other wars.

Union soldiers' graves in the National Cemetery are marked by the monument in the background.

When I first walked the cemetery grounds in late December several years ago, the sky was overcast, a storm was expected that evening. It was a good time to be alone in the graveyard— chilly, windy, silent.

At the north end stands an impressive monument, 85-feet tall and built of white Pennsylvania granite. It was erected in 1910 by the U.S. government to recognize the 2,436 Rebels who were buried in New Jersey's Yankee soil. The monument's granite tip points to the heavens, but the wide, multi-tiered base is anchored to the earth and surrounded by large, bronze plaques that bear the name and state of each dead Confederate.

The officers and enlisted men hail from such distant states as Texas, Alabama, Mississippi, Georgia, Virginia and the Carolinas. They seem out of place in this northern state, especially on a day when the blowing wind and gray skies intensify the cold. While they are remembered by name on the oversized markers, each individual gravesite will never be found.

According to Alica Bjornson, who at the time was Fort Mott's historic preservation specialist, the names of the dead Confederate prisoners were burned into the top of each wooden coffin, and a piece of leather was placed over the names for protection. The caskets were placed three layers deep, in large

The names of Confederate soldiers buried at Finn's Point cemetery are listed on the plaque at the base of the tall Confederate monument.

63

graves. But no one recorded the exact placement of the coffins. Fort Delaware records maintained a list of the names of the Confederate dead, but not their exact location. Later, the burial documents were used as the basis for the bronze identification plaques that rest at the base of the monument.

At the opposite end of the cemetery are Yankee soldiers who died at Fort Delaware while guarding their Southern enemies. The Union marker was erected in 1879, above where the 135 U. S. soldiers were buried. But only 105 names were available. These dead, too, are identified by a single, engraved, stone slab, now surrounded by a white-columned cupola.

In addition to another section with the graves of Fort Mott military personnel and families, 13 small, identical, round-topped stones mark the resting place of soldiers who are buried very far from their homeland. These are German prisoners of World War II who died while imprisoned at For Dix, New Jersey.

In life, the Yankees and the Rebels, the G.I.s and the Nazis fought on opposing sides. They hated each other; they tried to kill one another; they each fought bravely for their own sacred cause. Now, decades after their respective wars have been settled and, in some cases, forgotten, our country is no longer

Thirteen graves of German soldiers that died during World War II stand off in a corner of the Finn's Point National Cemetery.

North against South, and the Germans are considered among our allies. And all of these old warriors rest within the walls of a tiny, out-of-the-way, country graveyard, at rest together forever.

Contact: Fort Mott State Park and Finn's Point National Cemetery (entrance shown in photo at right) are located only six miles south of the Delaware Memorial Bridge, off New Jersey Route 49, near Salem, New Jersey. The park has an informative Welcome Center on the grounds. For information, call (856) 935-3218.

In this framed picture, General Zachary Taylor, in uniform, appears to be looking to his right. But squint your eyes and see if the mysterious skull appears, looking in the opposite direction.

'I Saw the Skull!'

*All of a sudden, this skull jumped out from the picture and looked
right at me! It was right there, for three or four seconds, I just
froze. Then I closed my eyes and looked again and it was still
there. I couldn't believe it.*

—Skull Man

Occasionally, an unusual incident occurs at Fort Delaware,
and it is so good that it becomes a standard feature of
each ghost tour. This is the experience that happened to
the person I call the "Skull Man."

During the first few years of the Ghost/History Tours, there
was a segment in the middle of the program when historian
Dale Fetzer would present a story in the administrative office. He
told a tale about the fort's commander, Brig. Gen. Albin Schoepf,
and the death of his daughter while the general and his family
resided on Pea Patch Island.

Since I had nothing to do during this portion of the tour, I
usually stayed outside, leaning against the white fence surrounding the Parade Ground.

I recall it was a very hot and humid August night, the kind
of evening when your clothes stick to your body. One fellow
stood out among the crowd of 88 tourists who had come over
with us on the ferry *Delafort.*

Encounter with the 'Skull Man'

He was tall, heavy set and was wearing leather clothing from
his black cap down to his heavy boots. Anyone dressed in that

cold weather attire was noticeable. Essentially, he looked like a biker, and I sensed he also might be one of those folks we sometimes get on the tours, who are inclined to make fun of the ghost tales.

While I was waiting outside for the historian to finish his story in the restored commander's office, the big guy came out of the building, alone. He walked directly toward me, shaking his hands and shouting, "I saw the skull!"

Thinking to myself, "Great. This guy is making fun of the tour, and he's decided to pick on me, because I tell the ghost stories. Swell!"

When I didn't respond, he walked closer and with his arms waving and stretched out from his body, he repeated, "I saw the skull!"

Figuring I had to say something, I replied politely, "Yes, sir. You saw the skull." I hoped that would get him off my case. By this time he was beside me, looked down into my eyes, and shouted. "LISTEN! I'M TELLIN' YOU, I SAW THE SKULL. AND I AIN'T GOING BACK IN THERE!"

Surprised, I realized this guy was serious. He was really scared.

With a dramatic change of attitude and genuine interest, I asked, "Okay, sir. You say you saw the skull. What skull?"

Lowering his voice, he turned and pointed back toward the room, where the rest of the group was still listening to the tale of General Schoepf. "In there," he said, then added, "It looked right at me."

"Show me," I said, and I turned and followed him back to the doorway, where he stopped.

"I'm not going back in there," the Skull Man said, nervously. But he indicated where the mysterious picture was hanging, so I could investigate by myself.

At first, he explained, the picture in the thin frame looked like an old guy in a uniform, staring in one direction. But then, he added, "All of a sudden, this skull jumped out from the picture and looked right at me! It was right there, for three or four seconds, I just froze. Then I closed my eyes and looked again and it was still there. I couldn't believe it. The third time I looked, it was gone. But I swear it was there, It was a white skull with two eyes looking right at me."

That's when the Skull Man left the group and came out to find me. "I figured I should tell you, since you're the Ghost Guy!" he explained.

Remaining outside, near the Parade Ground fence, he pointed in the direction of the room and urged me to go inside and see if the skull was still there, watching for him to return. I did.

Initially, all I saw was an old, black-and-white framed print of General Zachary Taylor, dressed in a uniform, looking to his right. But then, just as I was about to return and tell the Skull Man he was crazy (Well, I certainly would have softened my comment to sound something like, "I think, Sir, you have an active imagination"), my eye caught a fleeting glimpse of "THE SKULL!"

Redirecting my attention to the picture, I squinted my eyes and noticed an eerie face materialize—of a full skull. Its bare forehead and sunken eye sockets were looking out of the frame toward the right, or General Taylor's left.

It is one of the best optical illusions that I've ever come across, and I smiled as I walked back to the Skull Man to share my analysis. I also was pleased I could provide a solution to his mysterious experience.

The picture of General Zachary Taylor hangs in the administrative office, which has been restored to its original condition.

It didn't matter.

He didn't care about any "optical illusion" or "squinting eye" exercise.

His mind was made up. He had "SEEN THE SKULL!" And he wasn't going back inside for any reason at all.

In fact, he told me he wasn't going on the rest of the tour. He just shook his head and headed out through the sallyport. He said he was going "outside the fort," on the other side of the moat, to wait where it "was safe" until the boat arrived to take him off the haunted island.

Repeating the tale

Certainly, that story had to be added to our evening ghost tour program, and we repeated it on every subsequent tour. A few years passed, and one afternoon I was at a book signing in an area mall.

It was a very slow day. No one was at my table, and I used the time to grade papers and catch up on some reading. Then I noticed someone had stopped in front of my display. By the size of the shadow, I knew the visitor was tall and large.

When I looked up, a smiling, bearded face was staring down on me.

Immediately, a thought flashed into my mind, and I asked, "You're the Skull Man, aren't you?"

Laughing, he replied in a loud bellowing voice, "Yeah! And I know some people who've been on that tour, and I hear you been tellin' that story of mine on every tour since it happened!"

"It's a great story," I replied. "They love it."

Agreeing, he smiled. Then, he stretched out his arms and shook them in my direction, shouting, "AND I SAW THE SKULL!"

Meeting number 2

It was a summer Saturday morning in 2005 at the dock near the Fort Delaware Civil War Gift Shop. I had done the Ghost/History Tour the night before and was back in Delaware City for a few hours for a book signing.

I had about a half-hour to go. No one was nearby, so, as usual, I pulled out a book and began reading.

The sound of passing footsteps caught my attention, because they stopped in front of my table. I looked, nodded at the stranger who was looking at my display, and began to get back into my book.

When I realized he wasn't going away, I lifted my eyes, picked up a bookmark and began to offer it to the visitor. Suddenly, I paused. His face was familiar. We had met twice before, the last time at least six years ago.

I looked at his smile and asked, "You're the Skull Man, aren't you?"

Proudly, he nodded and we shook hands, laughing about our first meeting that had occurred so many years before.

He called over his wife, and the three of us talked, he reliving the experience, she recalling the embarrassment and I telling him that I had just shared his story the previous evening while leading a group on the island.

Before he left, he leaned toward me and said, "I got an idea."

I listened.

"The next tour, tell them you saw me again. That I'm still around."

I nodded, agreeing that it would be no problem to do so.

"But add this," he said, with a twinkle in his eye, "tell them you saw me at the end of the dock, looking out at the island. Tell them that it was obvious that I was still so much in shock that I wouldn't go out onto Pea Patch. That my wife was on the island, but that I was out here, walking the park and dock waiting for her to come back. That I am still afraid to go back—because of THE SKULL!"

We all laughed, including his wife. But as I waved good-bye, I thought: As I was talking to him, I had seen his wife coming toward us, from the direction of the arriving ferry *Delafort*. She had been on the island. But the Skull Man was talking with me. Maybe what he said, about never going back to Pea Patch wasn't a joke.

After all, he was the very first person who ever "SAW THE SKULL!"

The area near the Endicott section, called the 'dungeons' is one of the most popular and most frightening sites in the fort. Even during daylight hours, tourists have reported hearing sounds and seeing strange images.

'Where are the Dungeons?'

Fort Delaware workers and visitors have claimed they've seen a man in a gray uniform and long beard walking in the area of the powder magazine where General Archer was held.

Are there "dungeons" in Fort Delaware? The historians say, "NO!" They repeat the same brief answer so many times and with such force that it causes you to start to wonder if what they're saying is true. After a while it makes you begin to think they might be trying to hide the fact with, well, more and more "facts."

I tend to think that if it looks like a dungeon, sounds like a dungeon, smells like a dungeon and feels like a dungeon, it's a dungeon. So do a lot of other people who have never even used the term until they visited the fort the first time.

On several occasions, I've heard people say: "This place looks like a dungeon in an old castle" or "This place gives me the creeps. It's like I'm in a dungeon."

Well, they're not alone.

In fact, I bet Confederate General James Jay Archer sure thought he was in a dungeon, when he was sentenced to solitary confinement, living on bread and water, for three months during one hot and humid summer. To that Confederate officer, and other prisoners locked up inside the small, windowless, claustrophobic, damp powder magazines, they were living miserably inside a dungeon.

73

How the general got there and why his ghost might still roam the stone and brick caverns of the fort is an interesting story—one of duty and honor, or, depending upon one's view, dishonor.

Here is a quick summary of Archer's dilemma that led to his ultimate illness and demise.

The Rebel general was captured, along with his men, in the first day of fighting at Gettysburg, and he was not pleased. Four days later, he arrived at Fort Delaware and was placed in the officers' rooms above the sallyport.

Soon after his arrival, the general noticed that there were only a few hundred guards and thousands of prisoners. With the Yankees overwhelmingly outnumbered, Archer devised a plan to take over the fort and use it as a staging area to attack Washington, the Union capital.

At the same time, General Archer had been given the ability to roam the prison, after giving his word to the Union commander, General Albin Schoepf, that he would not try to escape. But the opportunity to take over the fort was too big a prize to push aside, and General Archer worked at his plan to overthrow the Yankee captors.

Unfortunately, someone who knew of the plan "ratted out" General Archer. Since a small amount of food could buy nearly anything on the island,

This small powder magazine served as General Archer's home for several months while sentenced to solitary confinement.

74

it isn't surprising that the Rebel leader's plan was disclosed. However, General Schoepf was more upset that his Confederate counterpart, in trying to escape, had broken his word—a high insult to the trust the Union commander had granted to his prisoner. Therefore, he sentenced General Archer to several months of solitary confinement, in a powder magazine on the southern end of the fort.

After so much time in that black, damp hole, Archer came out a broken man, sick with disease. He died shortly afterwards, and his family attributed the treatment at Fort Delaware as the cause of General Archer's death.

Fort Delaware workers and visitors have claimed they've seen a man in a gray uniform and long beard walking in the area of the powder magazine where General Archer was held. Ghost hunters who have visited the fort have gotten orbs in their photographs taken in that area. These orbs, some believe, are evidence of spirit energy.

Perhaps the broken spirit of General James Jay Archer has remained near the spot where he spent much of his quiet time at haunted Fort Delaware.

A lantern illuminates the dungeon arches. Orbs, like those shown in this picture, are captured in photographs taken at sites throughout the fort.

The 8-inch Columbiad gun, at the northwest corner of the ramparts, is the largest Civil War heavy artillery piece in the country fired daily. Its shot weighs 64 pounds, and the gun tube weighs 9,210 pounds. A firing demonstration is held during the day. However, at the conclusion of each ghost tour, the night firing is spectacular, and attendees line up to take photos and try to capture the 80-foot-long flame exiting the barrel.

Headless Major and the Man in the Black Cloak

Over the years, on many occasions, commercial watermen and also pleasure boaters have reported seeing lights on the ramparts —when no lights should be there.

One unusual Fort Delaware folktale is the story of the "Headless Major." A former worker on the island said he occasionally would experience sightings at dusk of a man in a Confederate uniform roaming the ramparts, with his head tucked in the crook of his arm.

While there has never been any verification of this tall tale, there is a related story, and a portion of it has been confirmed— by fort visitors, passing boaters and passengers, including myself.

Personal experience

People often ask me: "Have you ever seen anything at Fort Delaware?" and I used to say, "No." But that changed on a March Sunday evening when I went on a seven-hour boat ride with my friend and neighbor Wally Jones. This came about because Wally had an unusual job, he was a river pilot from the Pilots Association of the Bay and River Delaware. Throughout his career, Wally boarded ships in the Delaware Bay, off Lewes, and guided them into docks along the Delaware River, often in the area of Philadelphia. He also directed their return south, toward the ocean, after they had delivered their cargo.

He worked on thousands of ships, ranging from oil tankers to cruise ships and U.S. Navy crafts.

77

On this Sunday night, about 7 p.m., we boarded a container ship bound for Philadelphia. It was estimated that we would make our destination about 2 a.m., and I spent the evening on the bridge, observing the interaction between Wally and the ship's captain.

After it had gotten dark, I asked Wally to let me know when we would pass near Pea Patch Island. Since I had spent so much time at the fort, I wanted to see what it looked like from the New Jersey side of the river. Also, with the bridge of the ship standing about 10 stories above the river's water level, I thought I would see an interesting and different view of Fort Delaware.

About 11:30 p.m., Wally said we were passing the eastern shore of Pea Patch. He directed me to look out the window on the port (left) side of the ship.

I did, and all I saw was a black mass of land. Because of the darkness and lack of a moon that night, details on the island and the outline of the fort were indistinguishable—except for one glowing light on the ramparts on the New Jersey side.

I wasn't imagining the light. When I pointed it out to Wally, he acknowledged that he also saw it.

A few weeks later, when I was meeting with the historians at Fort Delaware to prepare for the upcoming season of Ghost/History

The ramparts on the New Jersey side of the fort go from the original buildings, on the left, to the Endicott section, shown at right. A moving light has been sighted on the New Jersey side of the fort.

Tours, I told them about the glow I had seen from the passing ship. I also asked them why they kept a light burning on the New Jersey side of the fort on a Sunday night in March.

Perplexed, they said, "We don't keep any lights on. We only turn on the

This view from the second level of the fort shows the Endicott section in the distance.

generator for the ghost tours. Besides, the fort is closed from October to April. There is no one here on Sunday nights."

Another fellow at the meeting shook his head and said, "There's something strange going on, up there on the Jersey side."

That's right, "Something strange is going on."

After that experience, I added this story to our Ghost/History Tour programs. Over the years, on many occasions, commercial watermen and also pleasure boaters have reported seeing lights on the ramparts—when no lights should be there.

Usually, off to the side and in a whisper, they mention "I saw lights at night coming from Fort Delaware. but I didn't want to tell anybody 'cause they'd think I was crazy."

Man in the Black Cloak

The following incident might provide an answer to reports of the mysterious light.

When we returned to the dock in Delaware City at the end of one tour, I was standing near the flagpole as most of the crowd began to disperse. As the tourists were beginning to turn away and head for their cars, two of the park staff that had worked on the island that evening called the tour group back and asked for their attention.

79

The workers wanted to know if any of the passengers had been walking on the second-floor level of the casemates (shell-proof enclosures) on the side of the island that faces New Jersey.

Apparently, several members of the tour group, and all of the staff who were standing beside each other at the time, did see a figure wearing a black cloak and carrying a lantern along the second-level restricted corridors.

The workers said the sight was both eerie and unnerving, especially when they confirmed that the entire evening staff was standing together. There was no way the mysterious figure could have been one of them.

The Man in the Black Cloak appeared again, near the edge of the Parade Ground. But whatever the unexplained object was, it apparently had disappeared before it could be approached.

"No one will get in trouble," a young worker from the fort told the group. "We just need to know if anyone from the tour happened to be up there with a flashlight or lantern."

Many shook their heads negatively, but I noticed that a few sported smiles, as if they thought the staff was putting on an act for the ticket holders' benefit. But, it was no show or game.

One of the young girls who had been working that night put her hands on either side of her mouth and whispered, "Oh, my

The Endicott section (right) is home to the area known as the 'dungeons.'

God!" as she moved her head back. Apparently, she was shocked that the Man in the Black Cloak could be a real apparition.

No doubt, some of the passengers were delighted that they had been so very close to experiencing a fleeting wisp of the netherworld. But for those of us who worked on the island that summer, this bizarre development was more satisfying than surprising.

Many, myself included, believe that an appropriate setting—that duplicates historic conditions—is essential to entice the spirits to reappear. Fort Delaware, isolated for more than a century on Pea Patch Island, does this better than most other historic sites.

About three years after the tours started, Impact Television Productions spent three days on Pea Patch Island filming the program *Ghost Waters*. It includes about seven segments from the most haunted water sites in the United States.

In Fort Delaware's portion of the program, there is a scene recreating the Man in the Black Cloak, who is shown walking on the grassy ramparts on the New Jersey side of the fort, carrying his glowing lantern. It's a sight that, over the years, some claim they have witnessed.

These guns stand atop the north end of the ramparts.

The 'Door to Nowhere' is the subject of much interest, and many legends exist about how it came to be and for what purposes it was used.

Door to Nowhere

When the Army abandoned Fort Delaware in the 1940s, some enterprising citizens from New Jersey and Delaware began 'visiting' Pea Patch Island, searching for anything left behind that might be of value and could be carted off.

For years, Fort Delaware visitors have noticed the door with no steps, nicknamed the "Door to Nowhere." As expected, such an unusual architectural feature has generated many questions and theories about its purpose and how it came to be.

"Is it true that the Yankees used to push the prisoners out the door and laugh when they landed below and broke their legs?"

"No," the living history staff members respond.

"Do blood stains from the dead Rebels appear on the rocks directly below that door without the stairs?"

"No," the historians reply.

"Did they hang the Rebels from that door and torture them?"

"No," state park guides patiently answer when asked.

So what did happen to create the usual setting that has become known as the Door to Nowhere?

Unfortunately—for those who like a good story about torture or murder or ghosts—nothing about the door's historical purpose comes close to satisfying their expectations.

Historical details

During the late 1800s, the fort needed to build a concrete section that would hold larger, more powerful guns that would be able to sink larger enemy ships.

83

This area, located to the south or right of the Door to Nowhere, was built. It is made of concrete and called the Endicott section. Visitors can see this large, newer structure running the length of the south end of the fort. It stands out because it is made of concrete not the brick used to build the Civil War-era sections of Fort Delaware.

But, in order to make room for the large Endicott section, engineers decided it was necessary to demolish a large building along the east section of the fort—where the Door to Nowhere still stands. This brick building was identical to the other remaining buildings in the fort that contain the kitchens, mess halls, quarters and offices.

So, the Door to Nowhere was probably the entrance to someone's room. Today, without the stairs, it goes "nowhere."

There's one more fact worth noting, and this provides the basis for a legend associated with the unusual door. After the Endicott section was built, the Army installed a metal stairway leading from the Door to Nowhere to the Parade Ground level, so the room could continue to be used.

A building like this one was demolished to make room for the concrete Endicott section. Notice the number of orbs that appear in this photo.

However, when the Army closed down Fort Delaware in the mid-1940s, during World War II, they took the iron stairs and directed they be given to the "metal drives," which collected anything that could be turned into bullets and ammunition for the armed forces.

From that point on, the Door to Nowhere became a reality. Also, if the door was opened and an unsuspecting walker passed through, he probably would end up seriously injured on the hard surface about 15 feet below.

When the Army abandoned Fort Delaware in the 1940s, some enterprising citizens from New Jersey and Delaware began "visiting" Pea Patch Island, searching for anything left behind that might be of value and could be carted off.

Fireplace mantles, iron stoves, doors, windows—essentially, any interesting and useable objects—were hauled to the island shore, loaded onto a waiting craft and spirited away. Eventually, the contraband was sold, junked or became a new family heirloom and incorporated into the homeowner's decor.

It's not unusual to be visiting a home in a nearby watertown and hear, "That's our Fort Delaware door that Uncle Chuck brought over from the island."

Legend

There's a great tale about a group of men who made several trips to the island and hauled off a fair amount of contraband. Unfortunately, one night a young teenager went "along for the ride." Of course, it was dark. Not knowing the lay of the land at the fort, and being young and careless, the boy ran through the "Door to Nowhere" and fell to his death on the stone surface below.

The fall alone would have resulted in a broken leg, but the accident turned deadly when the mantel that the boy was carrying crashed on top of the his neck.

The group covered up the real cause of the death and made sure the mantel wasn't left behind. After all, no sense leaving a perfectly good salable piece of history for someone else to cart off.

Eventually, through barter or as a gift or through an antique sale—the mantel ended up as a prized piece above a living room fireplace in a restored mansion in a Delaware River town.

Soon problems developed. The new owners discovered a small pool of water at the base of their fireplace, near the wall. After repeated unsuccessful attempts to find the source of the moisture they gave up and decided to wipe up the water every day.

They told the story to anyone willing to listen. Someone joked that maybe the house or wall was haunted, and that story seemed to stick. Through a friend of a friend, a psychic heard about the moisture coming from an "unknown source," and she paid the homeowners a visit. With nothing to lose, they let the woman into their home, allowed her to investigate the house and were a bit shocked when the medium grabbed the fireplace mantel with both hands.

"It needs to leave," she said. She added that if they returned the mantel to "where it belongs" the home's troubles would end. A neighbor who was involved in historic preservation suggested the piece might have come from Fort Delaware, but added that he wasn't sure, just offering an educated guess. But that was

Dan Citron directs AmeriCorps visitors to view the 'Door to Nowhere.' Over the years, this site has become identified as the source of a tragic death, ghostly experiences and a powerful haunted object.

enough for the homeowners, who removed the ornate wooden piece and dropped it off at the front door of the state park office, which at the time was on Clinton Street across from the dock.

Their problem was over, since the water stopped appearing at the base of the fireplace. But some think the mantel's mysterious activity didn't stop. It may have just moved to another more visible site—perhaps in the Fort Delaware Mess Hall.

Are there ghosts on the island?

Here is what Dan Citron, Fort Delaware's lead historical interpreter, had to say about history, ghosts and working on Pea Patch Island.

I feel that living history is one of the best ways to teach history. What makes Fort Delaware unique is that you leave the present behind when you cross the river. On the grounds and

in the restored acres, it is either 1863 or 1864 until you board the boat again.

One of the aims of the Fort Delaware Ghost Tours, besides entertainment, is to get people interested in the history that led to the stories.

I've never really seen anything that I could call a ghost. However, I've known plenty of people who have worked at the fort who also did not really believe in ghosts until they saw some things they had no way of explaining.

Dan Citron addresses a group during a stop in the area called the 'dungeons.'

DELAWARE CITY STORIES

There are many tales of unusual events in Delaware City. Some are associated with the fort and others are more directly related to the historic town. A few of these stories are presented in the following chapters.

Clinton Street Sighting

ometimes, I'll get a note in the mail, telling me about an unusual event that occurred during the ghost tours on the island. This, however, is a letter from a young woman who experienced her paranormal encounter in Delaware City, about 10 o'clock on a Friday night, after returning to the mainland. Here is her note:

My name is Jennifer. I spoke to you on Aug. 12, 2005, after attending your ghost tour at Fort Delaware. You had asked me to tell you about my ghost encounter in Delaware City. Well, here it is:

After attending one of your ghost tours a few years ago with a friend of mine, we decided to wait around and see if we could see any lights from Pea Patch Island. We waited for about 10 minutes. As we were leaving, we noticed a young gentleman walking across the grass in the park, from where we had gotten off the ferry.

The gentleman was wearing a Union soldier uniform and was carrying a musket rifle. I was a little concerned

because he almost walked right into the back of my truck.
It was like he didn't see me driving by.
My friend asked, 'Did you see that Union soldier?'
I said, 'Yes,' and when we turned around to see were
he was going he was gone.

The stores in that part of town were all closed, so we
know he could not have gone in any of them. And there
were only a few cars parked around the area, but he did
not have time to get in one.

It was like he just appeared, and disappeared.

Author's note: People wonder how such a sighting might have occurred. While there is no definite answer, it's possible that Jennifer's sighting involved an apparition from the past. The park at the end of Clinton Street, near the Delaware River, is referred to as "Battery Park." During the Civil War, Delaware City was a Union town, occupied by Yankee troops. The shoreline was reinforced with artillery pieces, and at the time it was known as "Battery Point."

Psychic experts say it is entirely possible for spirits from the past to reappear at historic sites. If so, the Union soldier that Jennifer and her friend sighted that evening could have been a soldier from the past.

This picture of Clinton Street, taken in the evening after a Ghost Tour, is where Jennifer said she and her friend saw a Civil War soldier.

This gazebo stands in Battery Park. This central site, on Clinton Street, along the Delaware River, hosts many of the town's festivals and events.

Curse of Newbold's Landing

Delaware City, originally known as Newbold's Landing, is a fascinating place with a colorful history. From its start in 1801, the area's founder, John Newbold, a New Jersey land speculator, believed his river site had excellent potential and eventually would have a bright future.

In the 1820s, when the location was selected as the eastern outlet of the soon to be built Chesapeake & Delaware Canal, Newbold's two sons laid out a formal town and dreamed that it would become a major city. Some suggested the location would even rival the larger metropolis several miles to the north known as Philadelphia. For a time, the Newbold brothers even considered naming their town "New Philadelphia," but eventually they decided on its current identity "Delaware City."

Like all towns, big and small, Delaware City had its boom periods when times were good. There also were rough years, when the economy was in a state of decline.

But if you step back and look at the big picture, "DC," as some locals call the small water village, might actually be cursed.

In the beginning, Delaware City was a big time fishing town, and there were processing facilities where river catches were cleaned and packaged for shipment around the world. Herring, shad and sturgeon were among the most abundant. Some Delaware City sturgeon roe was shipped to ports throughout Europe and even as far east as Russia.

But industrial growth, environmental problems along the river and economic changes caused a major decline in the fishing industry. Today, very few commercial fishermen work the river waters on a full time basis. During the 20th century, Delaware City's role as a fishing giant was dead.

In the mid-1800s, Delaware competed with Georgia for the

91

title of "Peach Sate," with thousands of acres of the succulent fruit growing throughout the state.

Among the most prominent peach growers were those located around the town limits of Delaware City. Major Philip Reybold and his family—who lived on the estate known as Lexington—cultivated more than 100,000 peach trees by 1845, earning him the title "Peach King."

But the blight came in the 1880s, and the peach industry was destroyed and has never returned to its glory days.

Now let's look at the Chesapeake and Delaware Canal. From its early days of planning—through its years of construction, to its opening in 1829 along the main thoroughfare of Delaware City—the narrow water passage was an economic magnet. It attracted thousands of workers, military personnel, travelers and tourists, the last group arriving to the area on excursion boats to marvel at the waterway, considered an engineering wonder.

Hotels lined the streets, restaurants and watering holes catered to travelers heading both east and west. Merchants and tradesmen swarmed into the town to make arrangements to ship their goods from Delaware City's busy port. Delighted shopkeepers sold their goods, and the economy of Delaware City boomed. Until 1927.

That's when the decision was made to move the entrance of the canal to Reedy Point, about two miles south of DC's business district. After that, the village was no longer as important a location for merchants and

Old Branch Canal near Clinton Street

travelers. When the canal's eastern terminus moved out of the town, a significant portion of the economic vitality drifted away, never to return.

So the fish are gone, the peaches are gone and the canal is gone.

All caused by circumstances and decisions made by those who were beyond the village's control.

But could the very area upon which the city rests be troubled, or "cursed" for some reason?

Could John Newbold and his sons, the founders of Newbold's Landing/Delaware City, be upset that their mecca by the sea never equaled the prominence and stature of Philadelphia, or Wilmington, or even Chester?

And, if so, could their disappointment and frustration have affected the very future of the village—or caused major decisions arrived at in the town to be altered because of a troubled, uneasy or negative force?

Possibly.

If so, this unseen power may have extended its influence into the very chambers of decision-making and had an effect upon the political history of the United States of America.

Think about this:

In the early 19th century, wealthy landowners and businessmen lived in Lexington, a plantation/estate located at the site of the current oil refinery complex, adjacent to Delaware City. From the verandas of the stately mansion they could see acres of peach orchards, pristine fields, riding trails and magnificent views of the Delaware River and its vessel traffic heading north and south.

In that era, selections of U.S. presidential nominees were made in smoke-filled meeting rooms. Wealthy and influential kingmakers, who were politically connected, often decided the candidates and the outcomes of state and national elections.

According to William Wingate, in his book: *Reminiscence of a Town That Thought It Would Be a Metropolis: Delaware City, Delaware,* a meeting was held at the mansion named Lexington involving the major decision makers of the day. Present, or providing input, were the Reybolds, Henry Clay, and several friends of John Middleton Clayton, a prominent Delaware politician who later would serve as President Zachary Taylor's U.S. secretary of state.

As the old story goes, Clayton was proposed to run as vice president of the United States in the 1840 election as second in command to William Henry Harrison, top candidate of the Whig party. Clayton said he wanted to run for president and stated he was not interested in the second place position. It was the top billing or nothing.

His demand would not be satisfied.

The other decision makers had different plans, and they informed Clayton that William Henry Harrison was their pick. Clayton could be vice president, they said, but he could not have the top job—at least not immediately.

"Wait until the next election," is what they probably told him. "Serve as number two for only four years, John, and at the worst eight years, tops. Then you can run for president and have our backing. Be patient. What's the rush? After all, Harrison is our man, right now. Take the vice presidential position. It's yours, John."

One can only imagine the prominent Delawarean's reaction. Impatient. Insulted. Infuriated. And perhaps even influenced by an unseen force. John Clayton flatly refused. It was the top job or nothing.

He left the meeting, annoyed that he was offered the second position, and that's almost the end of the story.

But there's just a bit more to tell.

William Henry Harrison won the election.

John Tyler had accepted the number two spot and ran as Harrison's vice president.

Then something a bit unusual occurred.

President William Henry Harrison, at his inauguration on a very cold winter day, spoke for several hours delivering the longest inauguration speech in history—and came down with pneumonia. Within a few weeks he was dead.

Harrison served one month—from March 4, 1841, to April 4, 1841. The president who gave the longest inaugural speech served the shortest term as president.

Vice President John Tyler assumed the nation's highest elected office.

One wonders what John M. Clayton thought when he heard the news of President Harrison's death.

If he could have gone back in time would he have made a different, more sensible, decision?

Would he have accepted the second place position?

And what if the meeting had not been held in Lexington, near Delaware City?

Is the chain of events the result of something more than just an "unfortunate coincidence?"

Perhaps.

And if so, some might suggest that John Middleton Clayton, who was a heartbeat away from assuming control of the Oval Office, was a victim of the Curse of Newbold's Landing.

Note: John M. Clayton's home, Buena Vista, is located on Route 13, south of the Route 40 split. The estate is named in honor of General Zachary Taylor's victory during the Mexican War. The 325 acres of land was purchased in 1845. The site is now a conference center operated by the state of Delaware. Clayton was born in Dagsboro, Del. He graduated from Yale University and became an attorney. He served as a state representative, Delaware's secretary of state, a U.S. Senator and U.S. Secretary of State. He died in 1856.

In the last years of his life, he probably often wished he had made a different decision at the meeting in Delaware City. If so, he would have been President of the United States.

Buena Vista, the former home of noted Delaware politician and U.S. Secretary of State John Clayton, is now a conference center.

95

Sounds of marching soldiers have been reported along Henry Street. Years ago, the narrow lane was an important link between the town and nearby Fort DuPont.

Sounds of Phantom Soldiers

During an interview in 1999, a Delaware City resident (who wished to remain anonymous) shared the story of the Marching Soldiers. He said the sound of bootsteps usually at night, had been reported being heard along Henry Street. The explanation, he said, is related to the town's location beside Fort DuPont, just across the south side of the Old Branch Canal.

"Around 1915," he said, "there was a swinging bridge that went across the old canal and connected the town with Officer's Row at Fort DuPont. Now, the thing was, the train stopped at a station that's gone now, but that was located behind the First Presbyterian Church."

The gentleman explained that columns of troops from Fort DuPont would march up Henry Street and then head east down Second Street to pick up supplies at the train station, and return to the fort.

He said there was so much traffic along their route that the government paved the two roads—Henry Street and Second Street—making them the first roads in town to be made of concrete.

The train station is gone, the bridge to the fort across what is now called the Old Branch Canal is gone and Fort DuPont is inactive and resembles a ghost town.

But some say the troops—or ghost soldiers—still march.

"I swear," he said, "I've had people in that section of town, near the Presbyterian Church and on those streets say to me, 'Hey, did you ever hear about the sounds of soldiers marching?' "

He said he's heard comments about the tromping several times a year. The reports never involved voices, only the steady sound of phantom footsteps, moving in unison, like marching boots.

"When they get up to look, there's nothing there. And the sound goes away," he said. "Then a few months later, they hear it again."

97

Fort DuPont

Fort DuPont was founded in 1863 to provide added artillery batteries to support Fort Delaware on Pea Patch Island. More guns were installed after the Civil War, and the site became a separate military fort in 1899. It was named to honor Rear Admiral Samuel Francis du Pont of Delaware, a Civil War hero, who captured Port Royal Harbor, South Carolina, in November 1861. This was the North's first substantial victory in the Civil War.

In April 1863, du Pont—who was a member of the famous gunpowder manufacturing family—led an attack on Charleston Harbor and Fort Sumter. Under his command were nine Union ironclads, including the *USS Alligator,* the Navy's first submarine, which was built in 1862, two years before the well known Confederate sub *H.L. Hunley.*

A statue (shown below) of Admiral du Pont stands in Wilmington's Rockford Park. Originally, it was placed in DuPont Circle in Washington, D.C., to honor his lengthy and quite distin-

guished military service, which involved service in the Mexican War, service on the *USS Constellation* and voyages to South America and the Far East.

During World War II, more than 3,000 troops were stationed at the shore battery at Fort DuPont. The site housed 1,000 German prisoners of war, most members of the Africa Korps.

Today it's part of the Fort Delaware State Park complex and has some recreational facilities. Many of the World War II era structures are closed to the public, and some state of Delaware offices are located at the site.

Body in the Canal

There was a time when the old C & D Canal seemed to attract bodies. Over the years, corpses—some the result of foul play—are said to have been discovered in the narrow channel.

On one occasion a body was found floating in the locks. When the coroner arrived he noticed it was headless and the top of the corpse was never discovered. A separate victim, at a later time, was found with several bullet holes in his chest.

According to Cecil County, Maryland, historian, Mike Dixon—a local authority on the history of the C & D Canal—in the 1890s a floating body stirred up the competitive spirit of two members of the local business community.

At that time, a town elected official and a prominent member of the town's fire company each owned his own funeral parlor. Upon learning about the opportunity to snatch a fresh body from the waters of the canal, the two men raced to the scene attempting to beat his competitor and claim the lifeless prize.

Historian Dixon does not mention which of the two undertakers carted off the floater, but his tale offers a glimpse into one exciting incident in the village near the waters of the Delaware.

A section of the original C & D Canal in Delaware City

Willis Phelps Jr., re-enactor and storyteller, stands beside the grave of an African-American, Civil War soldier, buried in Delaware City.

Lost Graveyard
Hosts Civil War Heroes

*The legacy—of those who knew . . . they had to fight to preserve
their family and culture and country—would be lost if we didn't
commit ourselves to remembering and to working to tell the rest of
the story. It's an important part of American history.*
                                                            —Willis Phelps Jr.

There's a picturesque waterway that slices through the
southern end of Delaware City, heading southwest, toward
the newer and much wider section of the Chesapeake &
Delaware Canal.

This waterway, called the Old Branch Canal, travels through
wetlands and marshes. During fall, the rural area features colorful leaves and tall, waving grasses that almost block out the
sounds of traffic passing only a short distance away.

Few area residents, and even fewer visiting tourists, are
aware of a lost cemetery, found relatively recently, that serves as
a final resting place for veterans of the Civil War—and what very
special soldiers they are.

To learn the full story I spoke to Willis Phelps Jr., 67, a
Wilmington resident and retiree of the Delaware Army National
Guard. But Phelps is more often recognized as one of the
region's most well known storytellers and as a noted historian,
particularly in matters related to African-American history.

Depending on the day of the week, or the place where
Willis happens to be, he might appear as a 19th century-era
blacksmith, a Wild West Mountain Man, a Seminole Indian scout
or a Buffalo Soldier. On this chilly, overcast November afternoon, he was dressed, very appropriately, as a Civil War soldier.

101

Our destination was an overgrown and nearly forgotten cemetery in the Polktown section of Delaware City, bordering the Old Branch Canal.

Among the tall grasses and mudflats we were seeking the graves of five Black soldiers who had served in the Civil War. Their distinctively shaped, granite markers displayed the initial U.S.C.T. (United States Colored Troops).

Willis agreed to pose for a photograph beside their makers, but first we had to find the graves. While navigating the narrow trails, he explained that the burial site was discovered a few years ago when a town official inquired about the source of a tombstone that some youngsters had found in the marsh and were carrying through town.

Eventually, Willis, along with Linda Beck of nearby Port Penn; George Contant, historian at Fort Delaware; and David Orr, a Delaware City resident and archaeologist; formed the Friends of the African Union Church Cemetery, in an effort to publicize the site's historic importance and insure its upkeep and preservation.

According to Willis, the cemetery dates back to the 1870s, and a least five African-American troops that served in the Civil War are buried there. They include

James H. Elbert, Company C, 8th Infantry

Alex Draper, Company C, 6th Infantry

Joseph B. Byard, Company C, 30th Infantry

William H. Crawford, Company C, 26th Infantry

Lewis Taylor, Company A, 6th Infantry

The grave marker of William H. Crawford, an African-American soldier, displays the U.S.C.T. designation.

"We call them the "Five Heroes of Polktown," Willis said, smiling. He added that they are some of the men who lived in the area and who went off in 1863 to fight in the war and serve in various units.

"This place is like many of the cemeteries that date from the Civil War," Willis said. "So many are lost become of their location and because the churches have closed or moved. Because this one is in a wetland, it is more challenging to maintain."

But even more important than maintaining the physical markers and threatened hallowed ground, Willis said, is preserving the story of those who served.

"The legacy—of those who knew, at the time, that they had to fight to preserve their family and culture and country—would be lost if we didn't commit ourselves to remembering and to working to tell the rest of the story. It's an important part of American history."

Willis described the existence of Polktown—"a colored village of the area," with "free folk and not slaves"—as very important, particularly with its proximity to Fort Delaware and its Confederate prisoners that were fighting to deny Blacks their freedom.

Anyone who listens to Willis, even for a brief time, can't help but be amazed at his wealth of knowledge and his ability to share it in an interesting manner.

Smiling, he said the storytelling skills started when he was growing up in South Carolina, and would listen to stories about his ancestors. Those tales left an indelible mark on both his mind and his heart.

Later, he discovered there were "Black" cowboys, and that

The hidden cemetery is on the north side (right) of this picture, showing the Old Branch Canal. Over time, some of the graves will be in danger of disappearing into the waterway.

103

realization sparked an interest in learning more about the lesser known—and lesser publicized—roles that African Americans played in U.S. history.

As an historic interpreter at Fort Delaware, and a sought-after storyteller who performs throughout the year, Willis said he often notes surprised reactions from his audiences—including laypersons and academics—when he shares his stories and information about Black history.

"Each time I will find someone very surprised or enlightened when they learn about how diverse American history was," Willis said. "That diversity, and those reactions, keeps me looking for more historical facts, especially in the local area. Our East Coast is a gold mine of information and the stories are waiting to be tapped and shared."

But along with the satisfaction of a responsive audience or uncovering long-forgotten stories, Willis said he's come across his share of surprises and disappointments.

"One lesson I learned," he said, "is the fact that Americans as a whole don't know their own history. I've been doing programs for audiences of different ages and I'll find out

Willis Phelps Jr. stands beside the grave of one of the Civil War soldiers from Polktown.

that people can't distinguish information from the Revolutionary War or the Civil War. Even some educators are surprised at what they don't know."

Some of the facts Willis has learned about Black Americans is that they

- Fought in every war in our country's history
- Were Mountain Men, who explored the West as trappers, explorers, settlers and scouts and
- Were brought to Fort Delaware as prisoners who had served in the Confederate army, working as blacksmiths and cooks.

"I'm always seeking answers," Willis said.

That often repeated statement refers to his quest to learn the stories about the five forgotten soldiers from Polktown, as well as the history and tales of prisoners, workers and captors at Fort Delaware.

"I spend a lot of time on Pea Patch Island," Willis said. "They say they buried some soldiers on the island, before they started taking the bodies to Finn's Point. Sometimes I walk the north end of the island, where it's quiet, and I'll sit and think and wonder what it was like for them, where they were buried and if there are any remains of them on the island that were left behind.

"I'm always getting questions, and sometimes I get an answer to the questions."

Author's note: For information on the cemetery preservation efforts, contact the following Friends of the African Union Church Cemetery: Willis Phelps Jr., (302) 429-0525; Paul Morrill, Delaware City Town Hall, (302) 834-4573; and George Contant, Fort Delaware State Park, (302) 834-7941. Willis may also be contacted regarding his performances via e-mail at Heritpro3@aol.com

Rev. Dr. Handy and the 'Weeping Tombstones'

Several years ago, I came upon the "Weeping Tombstones," standing beside Drawyers Church near Odessa, Delaware, For some time, I have been trying to find a reason to place this photograph in one of my books.

Thanks to Rev. Gary L. Baer, current pastor of Buckingham Presbyterian Church in Berlin, Maryland, I am able to use these eerie gravestones in this short chapter.

After presenting a talk on "Civil War Trivia, Legends and Ghost Stories" at the Berlin Library, Rev. Baer was kind enough to give me a copy of *Old Buckingham by the Sea, on the Eastern Shore of Maryland*, by I. Marshall Page.

Rev. Baer marked one particular section that refers to Rev. Dr. Isaac William Ker Handy, who had been the pastor of this particular Berlin Presbyterian church. But Rev. Handy also served for a time at Old Drawyers near Odessa, which is not far from Fort Delaware.

In 1862, Rev. Handy and his wife, who was ill, visited Delaware to see her parents. The Rev. Dr. Handy was an opponent of President Abraham Lincoln and Union actions against the South.

The gate at Old Drawyers Cemetery

Unfortunately for this visiting pastor, he frankly shared his thoughts on northern aggression to the wrong person.

As I. Marshall Page wrote, "In Delaware, he

The 'Weeping Tombstones' in Old Drawyers Cemetery

was treacherously arrested on the complaint of a fellow minister, whom he had befriended, and thrown into Fort Delaware as a political prisoner. He was Southern in his sympathies and, no doubt, proved himself too much in argument for the other minister as they sat at a supper table together."

During his 15-month confinement at the Union island prison, the Rev. Dr. Handy ministered to his fellow prisoners.

"He made the prison his parish," Page wrote, offering comfort to the sick and dying and providing encouragement for many and urging others to enter the ministry, which several did.

"Did the black-hearted scoundrel, " Page asked, "the brother minister who ordered his arrest while Dr. Handy was a guest in his home, do one-tenth as much Kingdom work in the time of Dr. Handy's imprisonment?"

Rev. Handy was so ill following his release from captivity that he did not return to his ministry for many years. In 1874, he published a journal, *United States Bonds*, about his prison experiences at Fort Delaware. He died on June 14, 1878.

Perhaps the eerie tombstones at Old Drawyers weep in embarrassment, for the treachery that occurred near their site, and for the imprisonment of a good man, who was the victim of a fellow minister whom he thought to be his friend.

No one will every be sure, but there has to be some reason that—at the top of the ridge, at the northeast side of the historic brick church—the Weeping Tombstones face toward the South, perhaps remembering the injustice done to a former pastor of the church.

OLDE NEW CASTLE STORIES

The historic town of New Castle, founded in 1651, has a strong connection with Fort Delaware.

The Arsenal at Old New Castle (shown above), currently a restaurant, was built in 1809 and served as a supply station for Fort Delaware. In 1831, when a fire on Pea Patch Island destroyed the old wooden fort, federal troops were housed in New Castle's Arsenal building. In 1832, the historic structure was used as a hospital during a cholera epidemic. In later years, the historic building served as an area school.

New Castle's
'Lady Along the River'

I remember thinking, 'Oh, my God! This is weird, very weird.' I also remember that its feet weren't touching the ground. It was floating about a foot in the air. And the faster we ran, it seemed to keep up with us.

—Donna Bowman-Petchel

There's a dark figure of a woman, dressed in black that floats along the banks of the Delaware River near New Castle. At least, that's the legend. And if you've ever walked the tree-lined, stone-covered streets of this historic Colonial-era village—in the evenings, when it's very quiet and there's little foot or vehicle traffic—you'd tend to believe the story is probably true.

But then legends are supposed to be associated with old places, particularly ones with historic markers, very old houses and centuries-old public buildings, graveyards and churches. While I had heard the story occasionally over the years, I had never found anyone who admitted they had actually seen New Castle's "Lady Along the River"—until I talked to Donna Bowman-Petchel and her friend, Carla Anderson.

Both women told me, without a doubt, they had seen the ghostly figure and that it had followed them while they were walking along the river walkway in Battery Park.

The incident occurred in the fall of 1997. A crisp river breeze, falling leaves and a chill in the air seemed to be the perfect time for the two friends to begin walking and running to get in shape. Donna said they had gotten into a routine, using the

109

path in Battery Park on the weekends and a few nights a week.

One weekday evening in late October, when it began to get dark earlier, they cut their walk short. They were both leery of going near the wooded area beyond the edge of the village—where there were fewer people and less lighting.

On this night, because, Donna explained, they tended to talk incessantly while walking, neither woman noticed that it had started to get dark.

Carla Anderson (left) and Donna Bowman-Petchel stand on the dock at Battery Park, not far from where the friends say they were followed by an apparition.

For some reason, Carla said, they both looked behind them, and they noticed an unusual shape.

"Suddenly," Donna said, "we both saw a strange object coming toward us from about 50 yards away. It was a dark figure that appeared to be in a cape or hooded sweatshirt, but it wasn't touching the ground. It kind of hovered above the ground and moved slowly toward us. We were both startled, and I said, 'What is that?' "

Carla saw it too. She said she didn't have any idea what the "thing" was. "But it was shaped like a person," she recalled. "At first I thought it was a person, but then it seemed like more of a blackish thing."

The "thing" followed the women for about 20 seconds, Carla said. "That was long enough to make us nervous and run away as fast as we could. The last thing I remember is that it flew off the path and disappeared into the high grass toward the river."

"It was freaky," Donna said, standing not far from the area of the sighting as she and Carla recalled their experience. "I remember thinking, 'Oh, my God! This is weird, very weird.' I also remember that its feet weren't touching the ground. It was floating about a foot in the air. And the faster we ran, it seemed to keep up with us."

"We still talk about it to this day," Donna added. "If I had been alone, I would have questioned my sanity, but because Carla saw it too, I was convinced that it was an apparition or something. And Carla's about as normal and levelheaded as they come. She won't even touch a glass of wine. So, I really believe we saw something unexplainable that night."

About two years later, Donna said she went on a Candlelight Ghost Tour with a male friend. That night she got a clue to the phantom's identity.

The Delaware River shoreline, along historic Battery Park, where an apparition is believed to have appeared

"We toured the City of Olde New Castle," Donna said, "and when we arrived at Battery Park, the tour guide told us about a dark figure that many people have claimed to have seen walking along the river in the park. Some believe it is the spirit of Lucy, whose young husband was killed by pirates just off the shore of the Delaware River in Battery Park around the late 1700s or early 1800s.

During more than 350 years, the cobblestone streets of Olde New Castle have hosted pirates, patriots, famous politicians, merchants and many of our nation's leaders.

"She was described as a 'pleasant-looking young woman with long, flowing dark hair,' and the couple had just recently married. After the pirate attack, the husband's body washed ashore three days later. For the next month Lucy walked up and down along the shore of the river. Finally, after a month of this, the young woman was so distraught that she hung herself in the woods of the Battery."

Even today, each time Donna and Carla return to the park to walk, the memory of the mysterious apparition is a topic of conversation.

"I wonder if she'll every show up again," Carla said, while admitting that she hasn't seen anything since that night. "I think about it a lot, especially when I'm here, but I try to block it out. I never want to see it again."

"I think I do," said Donna. "I'm curious and it's cool." Then, smiling at her thoughts, she added, "When we walk past the area, we call out, 'Lucy! Come on out! You got some 'splaining to do!' "

Donna said that soon after the sighting, when they were on the New Castle town tour, her friend wouldn't let her share her eerie experience with the tour guide.

"He said that everyone would think that I may have had 'one too many' at the restaurant before the start of the tour," Donna said, laughing.

For years, the two friends had different opinions about whether to share their ghostly experience with others.

"I have told so many people this story," Donna said. "And when I do, I kind of 're-live' the whole experience as if it were yesterday. Carla, on the other hand, has never told anyone, and I was surprised to find out a few years ago that she hadn't even told her husband. But she will admit to me, that she did indeed see the 'thing,' or Lucy, that night. There is no doubt in our minds that there was something out there that night."

The center of New Castle, close to the historic Court House, may have been the location selected for public executions.

Burned at the Stake
in Olde New Castle

After all, you don't waste these good burnings.

—Mike Dixon

You do the crime. You do the time." So said Delmarva criminal justice historian Mike Dixon, an expert on regional history throughout the Delmarva Peninsula.

To illustrate the meaning of this well-known proverb, he shared a story he discovered while combing the musty documents stored in the State of Delaware Archives. And what a great story it is.

In 1731, in the bustling village of New Castle, Delaware—then still part of William Penn's Pennsylvania—a murder attracted the attention of a bored populace. After all, in the days before DVDs, TV, movies, radio and even mass printed matter, there wasn't much to do in the colonies in the way of entertainment. Waiting for a traveling storyteller with a bag filled with puppets and a flute, or listening to local singers accompanied by a harp player would be the highlights of the month.

Thanks to Mrs. Catherine Bevan and Mr. Peter Murphy, her indentured servant, the good folks of New Castle were treated to an entertaining distraction—murder, trial and a public execution.

As historian Dixon summarized the tale—pulled from the pages of Benjamin Franklin's newspaper, *The Pennsylvania Gazette*—apparently, Mrs. Bevan enlisted the help of Mr. Murphy to do away with Mr. Henry Bevan, her husband. The two beat the man to death and stuffed him into a homemade coffin, figuring they could dispose of the body and tell locals that the good gentleman had simply disappeared.

Unfortunately for the plotters, the local constable happened to come upon the freshly constructed box, expressed his sympathy for Mrs. Bevan's sudden loss and then asked that the coffin be opened so he could inspect the body.

Reluctantly, Mr. Murphy pried off the lid, displaying the badly beaten corpse of Mr. Bevan.

Off to the town jail went the wife and her accomplice. However, more interested in saving his skin than remaining loyal to the scheming mistress, Mr. Murphy spilled the beans and was granted a lesser sentence—hanging. His evidence insured the conviction of the murderous wife. With some haste, to satisfy the needs of the bored townsfolk—as was the case in those days—the public execution was scheduled.

It may be suggested that the apparent unrepentant attitude of the wife played a part in her receiving a more painful and drawn out demise.

As the reporter for *The Pennsylvania Gazette* stated:

> *On Fryday the 10th Instant, Peter Murphy and Catherine Bevan were executed at New-Castle, the Man hanged and the Woman burnt, pursuant to their Sentence, for the Murder of Henry Bevan, Husband to Catherine. His [Murphy's] confession taken before a Magistrate when he was first committed to Prison, you may have seen in our Gazette of June 24. To the same purpose he swore against his Mistress [Catherine Bevan] at her Tryal. But before his Death, he declared that he had wronged her much, that she did not tie the Handkerchief round her Husband's Neck, and that the chief of his Evidence at Court was false; but that she was the Promoter of all that happen'd and consented to what was done. She deny'd to the last that she acted any Part in the Murder, and could scarce be brought to own that she was guilty of Consenting. Neither of them said much at the Place of Execution. The man seemed penitent, but the Woman appear'd hardened.*

On that day of the execution/festival, the vendors were out early, selling food and drink to the gathering crowd. The town center was packed with gawkers, from the aged to young parents carrying youngsters and newborns.

One can only imagine the tales of previous hangings and burnings of criminals that circulated through the crowd, which was hoping the current display would meet their lurid expectations. (After all, those who had traveled some great distance to witness the event did not want to be disappointed, particularly if the criminal succumbed too soon to the flames at her feet.)

Yes! It was a burning that Mrs. Bevan would suffer. No doubt, the eager mob whistled and applauded as the sheriff tied the convicted murderer to the stake.

Approving cheers roared through the mob when the fire was lit and flames began to spread. After what was deemed a decent amount of time, historian Dixon said, the authorities instructed to the sheriff to "strangulate" Mrs. Bevan with a rope, in order to "make her death more merciful."

No doubt, the crowed voiced its disapproval when the official moved forward to choke the life out of the murderer. But fate seemed to have a different plan, and one of which the mob, most certainly, approved.

During the effort to choke Mrs. Bevan, the ropes holding her to the stake broke and the woman fell forward into the fire. The flames, which had risen to full force, leapt up and consumed the writhing body. Mrs. Bevan disappeared into the inferno.

As the *Gazette* writer reported, "It was design'd to strangle her dead before the Fire should touch her; but its first breaking out was in a stream which pointed directly upon the Rope that went round her Neck, and burnt it off instantly, so that she fell into the Flames, and was seen to struggle."

When the convicted criminal's shrieking screams stopped, it signaled to those assembled that her death sentence had been carried out, according to the letter of the law.

Certainly, the spectators who had traveled by foot, horse and wagon to witness the burning had not been disappointed. As they departed the area, they compared Mr. Murphy's hanging, and the much more fascinating immolation of Mrs. Bevan, with other public punishments they had seen before.

When I asked historian Dixon where the burning would have taken place, he said it was not specified in the records and it would be hard to locate the exact spot with certainty.

I mentioned that New Castle has no "Gallows Hill" or "Gallows Road" street signs, like I had found in New Jersey.

Dixon said that if he had to venture a guess, the spectacle would have been in a central location, possibly even in the town square, directly in front of the historic court house. "After all," Dixon added, "you don't waste these good burnings."

While executions were believed to serve as a deterrent to future crime, Dixon said, they provided an economic boost to the community. They also were a diversion for the population that worked hard throughout the year.

"These burnings," Dixon added, "were largely restricted to women, who had been burned at the stake during the Middle Ages in Europe. The custom was brought over to the colonies and continued for a period of time."

The historian added an interesting hanging-related detail: He said a story in a downstate Delaware newspaper referred to the 1873 hanging in Georgetown of an African-American man.

"The locals were very upset that the law was changed in 1873 to change hangings from public to private events," Dixon said. "People had traveled from Delmar and Ocean View and Maryland's Eastern Shore to enjoy the spectacle and they wouldn't let them in. They were very upset, and it caused quite a stir."

Author's note: During one of our regular, early morning gatherings in Elkton, Maryland, at Butch Cubbage's shop, Picture It Framed, the New Castle burning became the focus of conversation. Present were Dixon, along with fellow Cecil County historian Milt Diggins, who serves as editor of the organization's *Journal*; retired Maryland Department of Natural Resources officer and Colonial-era re-enactor John Carpenter and his son, Chris. After Dixon related the details of the fiery execution, the question arose as to the type of wood used at public burning executions.

A few at the counter suggested that a hardwood—such as oak or cherry—would have been the Colonial-era sheriff's choice, particularly if the official wanted to treat the audience to a prolonged, well-done, drawn-out execution, that would entertain the viewers. On the other hand, pine or poplar, being softer woods that would burn faster and create a bit of a flash, would probably have been the executioner's choice, if he wanted to provide for a quicker, more humane, death at the stake.

The debate continued for some time and became rather *heated*, ending with neither side budging and, as no consensus was reached, it remains a *hot* topic.

Tale of
Tunnels & Treasure

Each day I read the local obituaries. It's become something of a ritual, done about the same time in the morning. I really can't say with certainty when the routine began. It's just one of those things that started up at some hazy point in time, and over the years has become automatic.

Certainly, it has something to do with getting older. After all, when you get to the age where there's no doubt there are fewer years in front of you than behind you, your outlook on life starts to change. Things that were so important even five years ago seem silly and trivial now.

Then there's the fact that your old schoolmates from grade school and high school are beginning to die. That really makes you stop and take notice. It always was expected that a growing number of folks your parents' age would be passing on. But when guys you played ball with and girls you dated and who lived up the block start to die, you can't help but pause and take note that the ageless man named Death could make a visit at your door any day, and when he stops by to call he doesn't leave alone.

But there was another, less threatening, reason for my careful scan of the obits. I was looking for a name, a rather unusual name. You see, it had been agreed that when I saw the announcement of this person's demise, I then would be able to share his rather fascinating story, and his theories, with you.

In August 2005, I read the notice of the death of Gideon Ashley Tibbadoue. There was no mistaking that name for anyone else. That's why he decided that the brief mention of the conclusion of his very long life would be a perfect way to let me know that I now had permission to share the essence of our rather strange and intriguing conversations and adventures.

119

The newspaper notice was very brief, only using up the three lines that this particular newspaper gives for free.

Years ago, young news writers would be assigned to ferret out the fascinating facts about the recently departed, calling their former friends and relatives, and then sharing the achievements and personal triumphs of the names set in formal black type. Usually, their final story would end with a notice of the date and time for the viewing and service.

Today, only small town weeklies continue this important practice and still consider it their obligation and a community service. Now, the bigger dailies give you less than a half-dozen lines. After that, it's pay as you go, and you can pretty much put in anything you want, after all, it's essentially a paid advertisement.

Mr. Tibbadoue didn't dish out anything extra. The notice placed by his hired attorney/executor stated the basics:

Gideon Ashley Tibbadoue
'Gyd'

Age 89, formerly of Warwick, MD, died Friday, August 12, at BelleVue Nursing Home. Services and burial will be private. The deceased had no surviving family in the immediate area.

Arrangements by

USHER HOUSE MORTUARY & CREMATORIUM

That was it.

Gyd, as he told me he preferred to be called, believed there was no sense making a fuss after he was gone, especially since hardly anybody bothered to take notice of him when he was alive.

He was what folks used to call a hermit, a recluse, and a cranky old codger that didn't send off any warm, fuzzy, "can't we all just get along" vibes. No, Gyd was more of a "get outta my way" type of guy,

My first meeting with this very amusing character occurred, I initially thought, by chance. Later, I discovered he has selected me to share his tale, and he had orchestrated our initial encounters with the finesse of an experienced, white-haired concertmaster.

I had arrived in Delaware City for a ghost tour on a Friday night in the summer of 2002 at 6 p.m., my usual time. I wanted

120

to be in place well in advance of the 7 p.m. departure of the *Delafort*. (The captain has a tendency to get a little edgy when we leave the dock late, and I had long ago vowed that I was never going to be the reason for his ship's delay.)

I was seated on a bench in Battery Park. It was in the shade, near the gazebo, just far enough away from the tourists who would be arriving for that evening's ghost tour. I used the time to catch up on whatever needed to be done and to enjoy a little quiet time before the show began.

Only about five minutes of reading time had passed when I heard an abrupt shout, followed by mixed frustrated muttering and swearing. Looking about three feet to my left, along the sidewalk, I saw an older man bending over, with some difficulty, trying to pick up a half-dozen cans that were rolling away, just out of his reach.

Placing my book aside, I grabbed three of the traveling containers and walked over to offer some help.

The older man looked up, nodded and put out his bent arm, indicating he could use some assistance getting back into an upright position. After a few words of thanks, amongst cursing

The park in Delaware City where I first met Gideon Ashley Tibbadoue

directed at "cheap paper bags" and the pains associated with old age, he began to head toward his truck. I followed, carrying my share of his haul.

With an abrupt word of "Thanks," and "Just toss them in the cab," he got into the old, rusted pickup, nodded and drove off.

End of good deed, and end of him, I thought.

Two weeks later, at the same spot while waiting to start the next ghost tour, he reappeared.

Same clothes, same guy—but with no grocery bag. He stopped directly in front of my bench.

I looked up.

He was staring me down.

I nodded.

He did the same and said, "You're that ghost guy."

"Yep."

"You helped me with my cans a few weeks back."

"Right again," I replied, waiting for him to get to the point. After interviewing people for years, you know when they want to say more. So the best thing to do is keep quiet and wait for them to spill the beans.

But he did the same—remained silent. He was waiting me out.

A fair period of quiet passed, and when it began to get too uncomfortable, I gave in and said, "You've got one don't you?"

"Yes," he said, smiling.

"Okay, what is it? Orbs, apparitions, footsteps, moving furniture, visits from little yellow men?"

"None of that nonsense," he said, shaking his head.

"So what then?" I pressed. Time was passing, and I was due at the dock for the start of the tour.

His eyes sort of sparkled, as he answered with a suggestion: "You guess."

"I did, already," I snapped. I was getting irritated and had a long night ahead. I still had to get my flashlight and water out of the car. I wasn't in the mood for solve-the-puzzle time.

"Don't get irritated," he said. "I got a good story. Real, real good."

Nodding, I forced a frozen, very insincere smile. After all, have you ever had someone come up and say, "I got a lousy story? Real, real lousy?" That's exactly what I wanted to say, but, sometimes you had to be nice, even to people who act like idiots. After all, this pest might be the grandfather of the director of state parks for all I knew, or the governor's father.

Instead, I said, "Great," trying to act "really, really" interested.

"Come on," he pressed. "Give me one more little old guess. Think bigger than ghosts, more fascinating, more real, more economically and historically relevant."

My time limit for enduring this nut job had expired. The Fort Delaware historian was at the dock waving for me to help him sign in the arriving group, and I had used up all my niceness for the week. So I got up and began to walk away.

"Sorry, I got to run. Got to get to work," I said, still maintaining a pleasant tone.

"Don't you want to stay and guess some more?" the old fellow asked, almost in a silly, mocking, singsong tone. It was obvious he was having fun; pushing all the buttons he could reach to shove me over the edge.

"Nope. Run out of time and ideas. Some other time, maybe." I figured that would end it. But not quite.

"Okay," he said, using that singsong tone while standing in place as I began again to walk away. "But you'll be SO sorry," he shouted, "because when you hear what this is about you'll be begging me to tell you all I know—especially because I'm the ONLY one left who knows all about it. But, that's fine. Besides, it won't be the first time you passed up a good story because you were bullheaded and stubborn and impatient!"

"ED! LET'S GO!" I heard the historian call in the background, but I couldn't let things go. This guy was really ticking me off. It was like he was reading from a script on "How to Irritate."

So I turned around, marched back toward him and snapped.

"Fine! What is so freakin' special that ONLY YOU know about it? And what makes you SO REALLY, REALLY sure that I'd even care what you have to say?"

A wide grin spread across his face, revealing nicotine-stained teeth surrounded by a white mustache and beard. "Two words, my young friend," he said in a voice slightly above a whisper. Then he paused and dropped them like a bomb falling out of the belly of a plane: "*Treasure and tunnels.*"

I heard myself suck in a breath of air. Instinctively, I replied, "Did you say 'tunnels?' "

He nodded slightly. My reaction satisfied him immensely.

"As in the *tunnel* from the fort to the mainland?" I added.

Holding his grin, he shook his head, indicating "No," then added, "Plural, my friend, as in TWO tunnels. I know where they are. I know who built them. And I know about the treasure."

"ED! WE GOTTA GO!!!" came the command from the dock.

I gotta talk to you!" I said, realizing I was showing a dramatic change in attitude.

"Fine," he said, obviously satisfied with his performance and his ability to slowly dish out the bait.

"Look. I really gotta go, right now," I explained, politely. "Can I have your phone number, so I can call you?"

Handing me a business card, he said, "I thought you'd never ask."

The black, block letters on the small card announced: "Gideon Ashley Tibbadoue, Delmarva's Leading Specialist and Consultant" followed by a phone number. The final line, in italics said: "*Call Anytime, I'm Retired and Make My Own Schedule.*"

As I looked up, he was crossing the grass toward his truck.

"I'll give you a call next week," I shouted.

"I'm sure you will," he called back with a lilt in his voice, certainly not hiding the fact that he had humiliated me and now was in complete control.

"Idiot," I whispered, describing *myself,* as I ran down the pavement to the *Delafort,* whose engines were rumbling impatiently. My wife is right, I thought. *I've got to be more patient. Got to listen before I cut people off, before I make abrupt decisions. Listen. Listen. Listen.*

As I arrived beside the folks on the dock who had assembled for the evening's tour, the historian said, "Thanks for showing up. I couldn't keep them entertained much longer."

"Sorry," I said. "I couldn't shake that old guy."

"No problem. I've been there," he said. "What was his deal? More ghost stories?"

"Yeah," I lied. "Another one with a tall tale to tell."

"Well," the historian added, "anybody that old must have something worthwhile to share. He looks like he could have escaped from the island."

Nodding, I agreed. "He did look a bit unusual. Well, I hope his story is as good as he says."

124

Laughing, my colleague added with a snarl, "Unfortunately, they usually aren't."

"I know," I said, and we turned and welcomed the crowd to Fort Delaware's evening Ghost/History Tour.

❊   ❊   ❊   ❊   ❊

For centuries, Pea Patch Island had been named repeatedly as one of the sites where Blackbeard the Pirate buried some of his treasure. Every few years, the *National Enquirer* ran a very poor looking sketch of the infamous buccaneer and, without much care, awkwardly pasted his image onto the shore of Pea Patch. The accompanying headline, read something like: "Lost Pirate Treasure Buried on Haunted Civil War Island!"

Each time the story and photo appeared, Delaware state parks personnel cringed for the expected influx of calls from treasure hunters requesting permission to dig up the historic Civil War site.

But, in this case, as with every legend and tall tale, there is a grain of historical fact. Blackbeard (Edward Teach) did sail the Delaware River. He did visit New Castle and Philadelphia. He did stop to see his mistress in a home in Marcus Hook, Pennsylvania, which is currently being excavated and examined.

And the well-known pirate of the Caribbean and Delaware Bay did hide from authorities in the Delaware marshes. One of his favorite hideouts was near what is now named Blackbird, Delaware. The area proudly proclaims the pirate's past presence.

But I was not at all interested in the possibility of pirate gold hidden on Pea Patch Island.

No, the old fellow's treasure temptation was not the real grabber. But when you talk of tunnels, well, that's a major issue of interest and one that has generated major league arguments among Fort Delaware historians, both professional and amateur.

Go up to an interpreter at Fort Delaware and ask them about the "hidden tunnels" and some of them will go ballistic.

I remember during one ghost tour, one of the historians was asked about the location of the secret tunnels that linked the island and Delaware City.

He replied, with words that went something like this:

"THERE ARE NO TUNNELS! THERE ARE NO TUNNELS! I REPEAT! THERE ARE NO TUNNELS from Pea Patch Island to

Delaware City! What do you think the prisoners did, dig 40 feet below the shipping channel and across a mile of water with SPOONS so they could WALK OVER TO DELAWARE CITY and escape? THERE ARE NO TUNNELS!"

He was almost out of control.

I don't know about you, but when someone in authority tells me too many times something doesn't exist, I start to think that it does.

It's like when your boss says, with added emphasis and a very fake/sincere gaze, "Heavens! Where did you get that *crazy* idea? Oh, my, there is NO WAY, we are going to move six other people into your private office." Or, "There is ABSOLUTELY NO PLAN to give you three times as much work to make up for the people who just quit. And even if we were *forced to do so* for a *very short/limited amount of time*, there is *no way* we would *not* increase your salary. I repeat . . . ."

When they repeat themselves, or when they go on and on—about something that's much more important to you than to them—you know you should start preparing for the worst.

As for the *secret tunnel theory*, I always thought a hidden passageway just might exist. I mean, think crop circles, and the pyramids and the Lost Dutchman Mine. They exist. So why not an escape tunnel from the fort to Delaware City?

Now, I was going to meet with Gyd and find out what he knew about not one, but TWO, of these mysterious tunnels.

Gideon Ashley Tibbadoue, "Just call me Gyd," said he was descended from a long line of landowners and merchants in Louisiana. One of his ancestors had been imprisoned at Fort Delaware. The young Rebel had escaped during the last year of the Civil War, made his way home and told the family an endless string of stories about his life as a prisoner for more than two years in the barracks on "Pea Patch." That's how the prisoner Tibbadoue and all his descendants referred to the island.

I met with Gyd frequently at his home, an old farmhouse he rented in the area between Middletown, Delaware, and Warwick, Maryland. Later, on several occasions, we walked the streets of Delaware City and areas of nearby Fort DuPont, looking for clues to the locations of the tunnels and treasure.

Being alone, and having no family and friends coming to visit, allows folks to live—as opposed to exist. There's no need to dress for success. No need to neaten up stacks of bills and mail, and there's no necessity to make use of things like shelves and cabinets. When whatever storage areas you had were filled up, there was always the floor.

That's the way Gyd handled things.

The entire first level of his house was accented with piles of stuff—papers, books, cassettes, video containers, newspapers and bulging file folders.

"There's not enough time to get anything done," he said, walking along and ducking down to avoid being strangled by the clothesline—that ran diagonally through an area that at one time had been used as a dining room.

Following him under the dangling obstacle, he turned, pointed to the papers hanging from clothespins, and explained, "Those are my important bills—heat, electric, phone, Internet. Can't let them get lost in the mess. Only way I can be sure they get paid is to hang them up where I keep running into them."

I nodded, thinking it was a clever idea. "Whatever works."

"Well, it works!' he said, as he pulled out a chair beside the littered table and used his elbow to shove a stack of assorted papers out of our way.

Grabbing another seat—that he had just cleared by tossing its mixed contents onto the floor—he said, "Get ready to take down lots of notes, but only after we agree on my rules"— which were pretty simple.

He would tell me all he knew, but I would keep the story secret until after his death. Then, when I saw his obituary in the paper, I could share everything he had told me to anyone and in any way I wanted.

"Preferably, you'll feature me in a book," Gyd suggested. "But you're the writer, so you decide if it's worth a mention. You see, I want time to find the gold for myself. But if I can't get the job done, then you can toss the facts out for anybody else who wants to try—or you can keep all this to yourself. It's up to you. But you can only share any of this after I'm planted. Deal?"

I agreed. There was nothing to sign. To Gyd, a man's word was better than a signed document. We shook hands on the arrangement. Then he got started.

He said his mother gave him the name Gideon. It had the correct religious tone, and she hoped it would inspire him to do good things, maybe even take up the ministry. But that was not to come to pass. This was no tea-drinking, Bible-quoting, Southern preacher sitting by my side.

"I liked the women, too much," Gyd said, smiling, "and the gambling and downing that throat-clearing moonshine. White lightning," he added shaking his head, "that stuff will mess up your mind. That's why I quit using it."

"When was that?" I wondered aloud.

"Which time?" Gyd answered, laughing a high-pitched chirp to match his rather thin, tall frame. He looked like a bearded sea captain and was skinny as a rail. "I think the next time I go on the wagon it will be like the three-hundredth time. But who's counting. After all, I'm too old for women, too cheap for cards, and I gotta have something to give up from time to time, so the beer and bourbon seem like the best options. You want a drink?"

"It's only 10 o'clock in the morning," I said.

"Looks like I'll be getting a late start today," he said, heading for the kitchen and bringing back a cold, light-calorie beer.

"Gotta watch my weight," he said, laughing, as he pointed to the label.

Did Rebel prisoners dig a tunnel beneath their barracks and the fort on Pea Patch Island? Some people seem to think so.

He went by 'Gyd,' to save time. Said he got tired of explaining his name to people who asked too may questions.

Over a series of meetings, I learned that he truly believed in the tunnels and, most importantly, the treasure. He had never seen either. But he knew they were there, and they were just waiting for him to find them.

"You told me you knew where they were," I said.

"So I lied," he replied, Gyd added, "sorta lied. They're like Antarctica or Australia, or God Almighty, Himself. You know they're there, because someone else has been there, seen them. You have faith in the person who told you. You believe them, and that's enough evidence to keep you going. In my case, that somebody was my granddaddy, Ashley."

Ashley Tibbadoue had been a private in the 6th Louisiana Volunteers. He was captured in 1863 and spent over two years at Fort Delaware. He died in 1889, but not before passing stories down about his miserable captivity and the Southern Railway and the tunnels that connected the fort to the mainland.

"What was the Southern Railway?" I wondered.

"The southward answer to Harriett Tubman's northward route," Gyd said. "The prisoners from the fort would escape through the tunnel, which led into the cellar of an old home near the water in DC. Then they'd wait there to get healthy—or be moved to other Confederate sympathizers in the town or area. Finally, they'd be shipped along the network in secret, back into Maryland and Virginia to get home or join up and fight again."

Apparently, Gyd's grandfather, Ashley, was involved in digging the last stage of the tunnel, which was finished in mid 1864. Before the tunnel, prisoners would try to swim off the island or hide in coffins with dead Rebels heading for burial in New Jersey. But the tunnel, Gyd was told, changed all that. Several hundred prisoners escaped during the year after it was built, and the Yanks on the island could not figure out how the captives were getting away.

"That's crazy!" I explained, telling Gyd about the 40-foot-deep channel that the oil tankers pass over, on the west side of the island heading to the refinery north of town. "The prisoners, even with machines, couldn't dig that deep. It's impossible."

Smiling, he calmly pronounced the words slowly, dividing the syllables. "Prop-A-gan-DA. MISS-in-for-ma-tion. Cov-er UP!"

"What are you talking about?" I asked.

Shaking his head, he snorted and said, "You been listening to them His-TO-ri-ans way too long. You sound like a Polly Parrot. That one tour guide in uniform over there, he just loves to tell that story about hundreds of prisoners on their knees using little spoons to scoop up tiny thimbles full of dirt. That's nothing but exaggeration for effect."

"Sounds sensible to me," I replied.

Shaking his head, indicating his disappointment with my comment, Gyd asked, "What do you think the prisoners did all day over there, sing in the choir? Take nature walks? Sit on their behinds from daylight to darkness waiting for a miracle? NO! They were soldiers. Trained warriors who had been in battle. They believed and were dedicated to the Southern cause. They got themselves shovels and organized, and they dug like both damnation and the devil was after them."

Gyd explained that there were 12,000 prisoners at the fort during 1863, and not all of them were as stupid as the Yankees, who won the war, now make the Rebs out to be.

"Remember this," Gyd said. "the winner of any war, he writes the history books. Them tour guides tell folks today how 'benevolent' and 'caring' that Union general who ran the fort was. How he treated the Rebs wonderful, like they were his little brothers and family members almost. They brag about how their death rate on Pea Patch was so much lower than it was down South in Andersonville. Hoot! They make it sound like them island prisoners had won themselves a trip to Disneyland

"Well, the way my granddaddy told it, and he was there so he should know, that Pea Patch wasn't no country club. They hung prisoners up by their thumbs. Tossed them in the dungeons for months at a time till they died from exposure and disease. Shot at them if they got outta line. Gave them the bare minimum to eat to keep them weak.

"Think about this, if it was so wonderful at Pea Patch, why did they try so hard to get away? Why not just wait out the war and eat good food and enjoy the good life the Yankees were giving them? No way was it a pleasant or even bearable stay."

According to prisoner Ashley Tibbadoue, the Rebels were organized into work parties and sometimes dug for up to 12 and 14 hours day. With only a few hundred Yankee soldiers to guard more than 10,000 prisoners—and with the prison barracks spread all over the island—the sound and sights of the underground excavations were concealed. There was no way the Union troops could, or even tried to, monitor movements of every captive.

But a nearly one-mile tunnel, under water would have to be an engineering marvel. I told Gyd there was no way it could have been done.

Leaning back in his chair, he crossed his arms across his chest, nodded and agreed.

"Then I'm right!" I said. "It was impossible."

"Yes, and no," he said. "And that's where we'll end it today. But here's your little puzzle to solve. There is a tunnel, part of it's still there, and when we meet next time, I'll tell you how it was done."

I told him I hated his puzzle talk, but he wouldn't budge. I left that meeting fascinated and still confused. But I was definitely eager to return the following day and get the rest of the story. And what a story it was.

❄ ❄ ❄ ❄ ❄

Gyd was wearing the same clothes, sat in the same chair and was in the same position as he had been when I had left the previous day. But he was holding onto a fresh, cold beer.

As soon as I placed my tape recorder and notebook on the table, he asked, in a tone indicating he didn't expect a sensible reply, "Got any answers for me?"

Frustrated, I said, "Ever since I left yesterday, I have been trying to figure out how they could move that much earth and dig that deeply in such a short amount of time. And I keep coming to the same conclusion: they couldn't, and they didn't."

"So?" Gyd pressed.

"So there's really no tunnel."

"Wrong!" he said, enjoying his ability to draw out his power play. "The answer is, they only had to dig less than half way."

I was confused, and I remained quiet. He was going to have to offer more explanations to explain his latest revelation.

Pulling out a stack of yellowed documents, he spread out a large map showing plans for the Chesapeake & Delaware Canal, dated 1820.

"Here is the original map of the excavation and elevations for the C & D Canal, beginning in Delaware City and ending at the Chesapeake Bay. They began digging in 1824 and completed the job in 1829. It was an engineering marvel. Follow me so far?"

I nodded and tried to rein in my imagination, which was struggling to race ahead and guess what Gyd was going to say.

"The big push, at the end, was to get the job done and celebrate this major success. They were digging like ants building a giant nest. Thousands of men, mostly immigrants, using shovels and hoes and buckets. Mules were dragging earth away and dying from the strain of their heavy loads. They had the best engineers of the time working on this project. When it finally was finished in 1829, what do you think happened?"

I didn't understand the question.

"What do you think happened to the workers?" Gyd asked, speaking a bit louder.

"I assume they looked for other work. No need to stay around when the project was over. They probably moved on, westward I would guess. They couldn't settle in Delaware City, unless they wanted to learn to fish or grow peaches."

"Or," Gyd interjected, "get hired to dig a tunnel to an island."

Surprised, I started to speak, but Gyd held up his hand.

To save time, he said he'd tell me the story that he discovered from journals, oral histories and other sources—including granddaddy Ashley—who, Gyd stressed, was there as a witness at the end of the tunnel tale.

Gyd sat back, took a sip of his beer and began

He said that a very rich, but still unidentified, landowner and merchant owned a decent-sized estate not too far from the water. The landowner came up with the idea of digging a tunnel to Pea Patch Island. He knew that the government installation was important, and that it already had a small fort in place. This wealthy fellow figured that if he could build a secret underwater connector to the island, he could get whatever price he wanted from the government and make more money than he ever dreamed of, even beyond his successful shipping/merchandising businesses.

The authorities could use the connector to transport materials and move troops during bad weather, and it also could be enlarged to hide ammunition and supplies. Plus, if the island was ever captured, it could be used for evacuation and later a secret invasion route.

What was most important was, at the time of his idea, labor was extremely cheap, since there were thousands of canal workers, mostly unemployed immigrants, who were looking for jobs. He also knew there was no rush to complete the job, since he, the island and the government weren't going anywhere. But the entire project had to be carried out in secret.

He hired about 80 men. Half would work part time in his orchards outside of town. The rest would dig the long tube, starting in the cellar of his mansion alongside the Delaware River. Since it sat on several secluded acres, either just north or south of town, no one would see what was going on. The owner arranged for the dirt to be hauled away or dropped into the river, where he built a dock for boating and fishing.

After five years, the tunnel was well along and progressing under the river, extending nearly a quarter mile. Another long portion was completed in the coming years. By 1840, he determined he was about half way across the river.

That's when operations ceased. He had been involved in previous dealings with the government and was not going to spend any more of his money unless he was assured of their interest. Also, he did not want to finish his secret project, only to have it taken over by federal authorities.

The gentleman went to Washington to get some indication of interest in his enterprise, being careful to stress it was only an "idea" and nothing more. He had several meetings with military, transportation and interior department underlings, who openly laughed him out of their offices, saying it was a "madman's scheme," that his plan couldn't be done and, if so, only a "simpleton" would spend that kind of money on such a "useless" idea. "Don't you know we have vessels that can travel above the water and carry any supplies necessary to the fort and its inhabitants?" he was asked.

Infuriated, he left the nation's capital city, returned home and tried to decide what to do next. The fact that his family was originally from the South—and that he knew that there most likely would be a division among the states over slavery and states' rights—helped him make his decision.

The creator of the first tunnel decided to continue the project, but at a much slower pace. Eventually, he believed, it would become a weapon in the war that was sure to come. And if conflict never occurred, he would use it to secretly get onto the island and steal government supplies and sell them back at a profit. The insults the businessman had endured in Washington, D.C., had stung him deeply, and one way or another he was going to have his revenge.

He kept only about half of his most trusted workers employed, paid them well for the continued secrecy regarding the project, and put them back to work.

Not too much later, when war was imminent, he informed Confederate officials about its existence, and he assumed they would use it to help launch an attack upon the government installation on Pea Patch Island. But aides to Confederate President Jefferson Davis had other priorities, and they put aside options related to the tunnel's use.

In the early years of the Civil War, both Rebel spies and engineers, posing as traveling salesmen and land speculators, visited the gentleman's home in Delaware City. They examined the now three-quarter-of-a-mile tunnel and were amazed by its size and sturdiness.

Did the ship channel near the refinery destroy the oldest part of the secret Civil War tunnel that originated on the mainland?

134

"A full-grown man could walk with only slightly bending," one Confederate military report stated. Another engineering inspector said it was "wide enough for men to carry a weapon and personal equipment with relative ease."

Since, however, the tube was not quite finished, there were no plans to use it to raid the Union coastal defenses on Pea Patch. Initially, authorities in Richmond decided that they would need to utilize a completed tunnel when the Southern Navy invaded Philadelphia.

However, when the Confederate fleet was destroyed early in the war, and the Delaware island was turned into a prison camp, the South's plan for the tunnel changed. Engineers, working under cover in Delaware City and as prisoners confined to Fort Delaware, coordinated plans to link the existing tunnel with a much shorter, second tunnel started on the island. Measurements and precise calculations allowed for a successful linkage with a relatively small amount of effort. Then, beginning in the fall of 1864. with the tunnel's completion, a series of large escapes began.

Pulling out a folded-up paper, Gyd opened it wide, showing a detailed historic sketch. The diagram displayed the entire island, along with the location of the main fort, surrounded by the moat, and hundreds of buildings scattered across Pea Patch. Passing over the hospital area, guardhouses and stables, his hand stopped and he pointed a finger on the west side of the interior of the fortress, slightly north of the walkway crossing the moat.

"The tunnel's entry point on Pea Patch was a damaged and, therefore, empty cistern," said Gyd. "It was in the bottom of the structure, below this kitchen, near the northwest side of the fort's walls. The underground area was huge, about 40 feet wide and very high. Prisoners would be working inside the fort and then just, sort of, 'disappear.' They entered beneath the stone floors through secret passages in several closets. Once they were through the cistern they walked along a narrow tunnel to the area below the prison barracks. The Rebel camp was just a hop and skip away, covering the entire west side of the island. Then the escapees would walk, without care or any threat, all the way under the river. That's where it got wide enough to pull a wagon through. And that passageway went directly over to DC.

"They said if you were in the camp and if you heard somebody whisper it was 'Time to take *your River Walk'* then it would be your turn to leave the place. And according to Confederate military records, quite a lot of them did."

Gyd explained that Rebel officers on Pea Patch had to be very careful that they didn't empty the fort of too many men at one time. Naturally, everyone who worked on the digging wanted out, and they were among the very first to go. Later, small groups would be allowed to get away, but only following a slow and structured schedule.

Although amazed, I told Gyd I had a few questions, such as: Where is the house and source in Delaware City?

What about the deep refinery ship channel? and

Doesn't the government know about this and why continue the cover up?

Gyd had asked himself the same questions, and he had his answers ready.

The ship channel wasn't there during the Civil War. The refinery wasn't there until after World War II, so the tunnel existed for nearly a hundred years unmolested. But when they dredged the river bottom to create the deep channel for the tankers, it cut the original tunnel right down the center. There's the second section that's still on the island, under the fort, and there's the other, original portion, that starts from the still undiscovered source in Delaware City. It has to be close to town, somewhere along the coastline.

After all his years of searching, Gyd said he had not found the location of the house where the tunnel starts. It could have been where the refinery stands and be long gone. It could be one of the old homes still standing, and it could be under the wooded area that has grown up on the edge of town. It might even be on Fort DuPont. Locating the original tunnel has been his unfinished quest for more than 20 years.

"As for the cover up," he said, "well, that has to do with the lost treasure."

"I'm not really interested in hearing any Blackbeard stories," I said,

Gyd looked annoyed, shook his head and snapped, "You're the one who keeps bring up the pirate, not me. Have I ever mentioned his name to you, even once? Have I?"

I realized he was right. He never talked about the famous pirate. That had been me.

"Right!" he agreed. "I'm talking about *real* gold. *Rebel* gold that was bound from Philadelphia to Richmond in early 1865 and that I was told is still hidden in the tunnel that ran from DC to the island. My granddaddy told my daddy, who told the story to me. He said that Ashley Tibbadoue himself helped haul that gold off a boat and bury it in the ground somewhere in the tunnel."

"Wait a minute," I said, entirely surprised. "Back up and fill me in on this one. Because this is all new to me."

"Gladly," Gyd said, again sporting a self-satisfied smile, "after I have another beer. You want one now?"

"Yeah," I said, "and let's add a shot of bourbon to that."

"Now you're talking," Gyd said, and he came back, put the bottles on the table and began what was perhaps the most interesting part of his story.

Most people, Gyd said, think that the country was strictly divided between slave and free, North and South along the Mason-Dixon Line. This famous boundary, basically, is between Maryland and Pennsylvania. But there were many Southern sympathizers and spies living throughout the northern states. There were draft riots in New York City, and Confederate agents worked in most of the major Northern cities, trying to get foreign governments to recognize the independence of the South and support the Confederate government. And, as in all wars, money was very important.

A shipment of gold was heading for Richmond, but it never arrived. Fearing capture, the ship pulled into Delaware City, posing as a merchant freighter loaded with textiles, and the goods were unloaded and taken to the mansion where the end of the tunnel was located.

"My granddaddy said they took nearly 40 heavy, wooden crates off that ship. The boxes, marked "MACHINERY," but filled with gold, were loaded onto wagons, right under the Yankees' noses, and hauled out to that estate. Some of the treasure was buried on the grounds and some was carried into the tunnels and covered up in holes close to the shore. But it was still there when the war was over. My granddaddy, Ashley, said he saw it with his own eyes, 'cause he was there the day the war ended and there was no need to send it any farther south."

"So," I said, "if this is true, the owner of the place probably dug it up and kept it for himself."

"Good thought," Gyd said, "but my granddaddy Ashley was there when the Yanks surrounded the mansion, after they found out about the tunnel. The owner got in a waiting boat and escaped with the clothes on his back and a handful of his men, including my granddaddy. The bossman never came back. He died down South, rather suddenly. And as far as I could figure, nobody was left in town who knew the gold was left behind."

Still not convinced, I said, "So you actually think that this gold is sitting there, after 140 years?"

"Why not?" Gyd asked, calmly. "Sure could be. Besides, I figure it's probably worth 10, maybe 20 million today. Wouldn't you think that much money should be worth trying to find? In my mind it's a better hobby than collecting stamps or playing the slots. All we have to do is find the right spot, put a couple of shovels in the ground and see what we find—but the key is to do it without raising suspicion. That, my newfound friend, is why it's taken me about 20 years of scouting and sniffing around, with no results. But I'm not giving up yet. Still got a few good years left to keep up the hunt."

Some believe the abandoned, old coastal defenses at Fort DuPont might conceal the mainland entrance to the mysterious tunnel.

I gave him a question-mark look, mentioning that two decades of looking with no results ought to give him the idea that he was on a wild goose chase.

But he had an answer.

Gyd explained that over the years he's been checking real estate records, court documents, been in every house in Delaware City that's gone up for sale, spoken to fishermen and hired them to sail him up and down the coastline, so he could take "nature pictures."

"You don't understand," Gyd said, with a weary tone of disappointment that he had to take time to explain what he considered to be obvious. "It wasn't like this was my full-time, 9-to-5 job. I didn't go house to house with a clipboard and map, checking off a long list and dangling it out for all to see. You gotta be cagey about it, especially in a small town like this. They got people here with nothing to do but watch the trash truck and see if there's a new worker on the back.

"I'd watch out for a new sale sign here, an open house there. I'd check out a boarded-up, vacant shack on occasion. Pose as a birder or arrowhead hunter. If there was a work crew digging up a sewer line or putting in a new road, I'd talk to the guys during their breaks, while they were resting on the side of the curb. Start up a conversation with somebody who was doing some remodeling work in the old houses. Stuff like that. Never anything obvious."

Then there was the refinery. But Gyd seemed to have had that covered, too.

"I been in there, at nights, mostly. Talk about a spooky place, with strange smells and flames shooting off strange glows. I didn't like those excursions. But you'd be surprised how easy it is to bribe a guard making $8 an hour," he said. "So far, no luck. I'm even beginning to think of starting to look south of town, in and around old Fort DuPont. I've pretty much played out the north side of DC. I don't know. But I'm too old to give up, or too stubborn or stupid. You can take your pick. So there's the whole story, at least the main parts. And that brings me to you."

"So where do I come into your master plan? You said you want me to write your theory, your granddaddy's tall tale, right?"

"That's right," Gyd said, "but in the meantime, I figured I could use a colleague to continue my exploration. Together, we'd be able to cover more ground. I'd also enjoy having the chance to have somebody to bounce ideas off of, share what I've already done. What do you think?"

"You want me to go treasure hunting with you?"

"Sort of. You can come and poke around with me. You know a lot of those fort people. Figured you might be able to get us into some places that are closed to the public, but without letting anybody know what's really going on."

Hesitant, I tried to put off making any quick decision. Instead, I asked, "So you want me to help you steal this gold mine of lost treasure from the fort and state of Delaware?"

"Look," Gyd said, shaking his head, obviously annoyed, "they've had about a century and a half to come up with the stuff. How much more time do you think I should give them? I mean, I know government work moves at a slow pace, but at this point, it's finders keepers—and I aim to be the finder. So make up your mind. You want in or not?"

I wasn't thrilled with the idea. So I dodged him a second time. He read my non-reply and eventually stopped pressing me about the offer to be involved actively in his quest.

This picture of the Parade Ground at Fort DuPont was found in Gyd's files. Could it be a clue to the location of the rumored tunnels?

But we kept in touch and took some walks together.
I visited him at his place a few times a year, got the latest
updates on his roamings and pokings. More importantly, I
learned quite a bit more about the area. He had done considerable research—enough to make serious historians look inept.

Gyd said people in the government—state and feds—knew
about the tunnel. They'd kept it a secret; even a select few had
been inside. But they never realized they had walked right over
and around the Confederate gold.

"No way they don't know about that tunnel," Gyd said. "I
heard they were using it during World War I and WW II, when
the army was still over there, before the channel dredging cut it
in half. They didn't let it be known, but they put it to good use.
Hiding stuff like important papers, and they brought a lot of
prisoners there during the big war. Took them down there in
that hole and scared them to death. Used it for secret interroga-
tions. Later they even used a bunch of the German prisoners
from Fort DuPont for upkeep of the buildings on the island and
also shoring up the insides of the tunnel."

Gyd said, "Using them Germans was smart. After all who
were they gonna tell, and who'd understand what they were talking about if they tried to say anything about the passageway?"

"But as for the existence of the treasure, that's not common
knowledge. It's like they're sitting on a gold mine and don't
even know it." Laughing, Gyd added, "They're so worried about
building up the town's tourism, thinking that one-day visitors
will be their golden calf, and they got a pot load of the real stuff
sitting in the ground, just waiting to be found. That's sorta funny,
don't you think?"

I nodded and started to dream what it would be like to find
$20 million in gold. Historically, it would be very interesting.
Financially, it would be life changing. But, like I said, spending
weekends roaming the town with Gyd, stomping in the marshes
looking for a a spot to dig a hole in the ground wasn't for me.

Eventually, Gyd had to give up the hunt. The old body parts
only last so long, and his mind couldn't make his old engine get
up and go. He told me he was heading to a nursing home, and
he only had so much space in his small half of a room. Would I
come over and take some of the old relics he had collected over
the years off his hands?

Of course, I agreed.

When I arrived, he was sitting in a wheelchair, waiting for a final ride from his house of many years. Stacked on his porch were three cardboard boxes, each with my name neatly marked on the sides and tops.

"Look at them when you get home, whenever you got nothin' to do. I didn't have anybody else to give them to," Gyd said. "Besides, them nosy attendants and nurses would probably root through my stuff and steal me blind. Better to toss it your way. Do what you want with it."

I said, "Thanks" and "Good-bye," and I restated our deal—that I would tell his story after he was in a better place, where his real lasting treasure would be life in a better eternal world.

He looked at me and smiled, "Or, you could keep my story all to yourself and keep looking for the big stash. It would be big time news, finding that much gold in that sleepy old town by the sea."

I started to speak, to decline again, when he put up his hand. "I know. You're a busy man. No time to treasure hunt. But think about it. If you find it, it'd be like we did it together."

I laughed and packed the boxes in my car. Turning back toward his porch for a final look. I saw him smile and offer a weak wave. "Get goin'," he commanded, "I got more important stuff to do."

"I'll stop by your new place!" I shouted.

He didn't reply and slammed the front screen door.

I never made it there. Gyd passed away within a month of the move.

He probably willed himself to die. Being independent for that long, most likely he couldn't bear the restrictions and lousy, healthy food and strange roommates and the routine, dull, end-of-life-style of living.

On that day I read his obit, I realized that I had never found the time to go through his boxes. I felt guilty. He had thought enough to give me his most prized possessions, and I had put them aside, forgetting about Gyd and his life's obsession.

Later that day I pulled out the three still-sealed, cardboard cases. Many of the items were familiar—his maps and notes, the diary he kept that listed the addresses of homes or businesses he had been in. There also were details that he had thought were important discoveries during his interviews. Old pictures of the streets of Delaware City filled one folder, plus images taken during the Civil War. There also were turn-of-the-19th-century pictures and even more modern, color ones of relatively recent trips he had made to Fort DuPont and Fort Delaware.

There was really nothing new—except a brown manila, legal-size envelope closed tightly with clear, wide tape.

My name was on the front in simple, printed letters. The initials weren't written with a thick or bold stroke, suggesting Gyd had sealed it when he was getting weak, probably just before our final meeting.

I shook the thin parcel and felt something heavy move inside, slamming against the sides of the brown paper container.

After ripping the seal, I turned it over, and a coin fell onto my desk. It was gold. Fat, flat and heavy, it hit the wooden desktop with a clunk. "Carolina Gold, August 1, 1834" was imprinted on one side. The reverse stated in raised letters: "C. Bechtler 5 Dollars."

A single page of white paper, with a very short note was in my hands. A second typed sheet with some information was attached with a staple. The brief message read:

> *My Dear Young Friend:*
> *Here is a little prize. A beautiful, Bechtler $5 gold piece for your consideration. The current value of this rather unique gift could be worth investigating, and it is given with the delightful hope of driving you crazy with questions. You see, it might be a rare piece that I had purchased from a numismatic dealer (read the document attached to this note). Or it just might be a solitary sample of the real cache of long-sought treasure that I had discovered in the last year of my lengthy search.*
> *The choice is up to you. (But it is not my goal in life to make your decision in this matter of my treasure quest an easy one.)*
> *If you decide this coin is from the hoard and, therefore, you plan to continue my search, I guarantee it is worth your effort. For if this single small piece of wealth was really the result of my discovery, there's so very much more where it came from.*

*And if it's all simply a grand and rather expensive
ruse, well, then I'll enjoy the aggravation I put you and
others through—as I watch your frustration from my
perch up here, or, more likely, from a more heated location down below.*

*You were kind to endure an old man's stories, and I
enjoyed your company. Certainly, I wish you well.*

*Until we meet again, in a better place than where I
saw you last,*

Good luck and watch your back,

Gyd

So ends Gyd's treasure tale, at least his active part of his
rather fascinating story.

After reading my late friend's added enclosure, I learned that
the Bechtler coin that he left me was minted—along with many
thousands of others—in Philadelphia for a respected Southern
gold dealer named Christian Bechtler. The noted jeweler would
send gold—received from North Carolina miners, who were his
clients—to the northern city to be minted.

The jeweler directed the precious metals be formed into special coinage in the nation's first mint, in Philadelphia. Over the
years, from 1831 to 1857, the Bechtler family business minted
untold small fortunes in coins, which were well respected for
their precious metal content and design.

Gyd's research seems to have indicated that Bechtler's coins
probably were hoarded by Southern sympathizers living in
Pennsylvania, In early 1865, the gold was collected and being
transported by sea to the South. When the ship captain discovered his cargo was in danger of being intercepted by Union
ships at the mouth of the Delaware Bay, he changed course.
Rebel sympathizers decided to hide the cases of gold—that they
had hoped would help sustain the Southern war effort—in
Delaware City, a well known Confederate stronghold.

I looked up Bechtler gold coins on the Internet, and found
out that old Gyd had left me the real thing, with a possible value
of several thousand dollars.

But more than being a pricey gift, it's become a final thorn
in my side, a bothersome clue in the back of my mind. You see,

it is constantly whispering that Gyd had been right, and that he might have found the long lost pot of gold he had been seeking.

And if he did, then the bulk of the treasure is still hidden in that remaining section of the lost tunnel—the tunnel that fort employees, area historians and locals all swear on a stack of *Bibles* "does not exist."

So I ask you: Whom would you believe?

A colorful character that followed a dream, based on trusted testimony of a family member? Or would you accept the spin, perfected by an endless line of state and federal bureaucrats, whose primary job is to mock the efforts of romantic searchers and cast their dreams and stories in a bad light?

I guess I'm inclined to put my money on Gyd, besides, it's a lot more fun to chase a rainbow.

But, to be honest, if Ashley Tibbadoue's buried Rebel gold is still hidden around Delaware City, it's something we'll probably never hear about.

After all, if you found $20 million in buried treasure would you tell anyone?

Uncle Sam would tax you to death. Officials would try to lay claim to your find, calling it "state property." You'd hear from useless relatives you never knew existed. And a long line of charlatans, inventors and schemers would be hot on your heels, trying to pick you clean of whatever portion of the gold you were able to salvage.

Who needs the aggravation?

Who needs to be that rich?

Still, it would be exciting to walk into that long lost tunnel and have a look around. There must be so many ghosts and secrets and stories waiting to be found.

So if you're inclined to take up Gyd's search, good luck. Buy a sturdy shovel, and, please, keep the results of your adventures to yourself.

Author's note: The events and characters in this Legend and Lore story are fictitious. Certain real locations and composites of historical persons are mentioned, but all of the other events, people and ideas in this tale are strictly imaginary. Despite this statement, a few of our proofreaders still believe hidden Confederate gold and secret tunnels might just exist somewhere near Delaware City. What do you think?

About the Author

Since 1997, Ed Okonowicz has helped guide Fort Delaware's popular Ghost/Lantern History Tours, which he co-developed with Lee Jennings, Delaware state parks historian.

Ed is a Delaware native, an award-winning storyteller and a regional author of more than 20 books on Delmarva culture and oral history and mid-Atlantic folklore. As an adjunct instructor, he teaches journalism, folklore, talk radio and storytelling courses at the University of Delaware, where he worked for 21 years as an editor. *Civil War GHOSTS at Fort Delaware*, published in the spring of 2006, is his most recent book.

Since 1979, he has written more than 1,000 articles for such regional publications as the *Wilmington News Journal, Cecil Whig, Delaware Today* and *Chesapeake Life*. He currently writes columns for *Nor'easter* and *Cecil Soil* magazines. In 2005, he was named Best Delaware Local Author in the Readers' Choice Awards poll, sponsored by *Delaware Today* magazine.

He has served on the Maryland State Arts Council Traditional Folk Arts Advisory Panel and is a member of the Delaware Humanities Speakers Bureau and Visiting Scholars Program and the Maryland Humanities Council Speakers Bureau.

In October 2005, he appeared as an expert on The Learning Channel in *Possessed Possessions*, a two-hour, *Antiques Roadshow*-type program featuring haunted objects and collectibles. (He has written two books on this topic.)

Ed presents programs and talks on a variety of topics, including area history and folklore, throughout the mid-Atlantic region, and he also presents a number of school programs. Details on his books, programs, tours and activities can be found on his web site, at www.mystandlace.com

Ed's wife, Kathleen Burgoon Okonowicz, creates the covers, design and layout for Ed's books. She is a signature member of the Baltimore Watercolor Society and has exhibited her original watercolors in shows throughout Maryland and Delaware.

Kathleen's work can be seen on her website: www.mystandlace.com/gallery.html

146

Baltimore Ghosts
History, Mystery, Legends & Lore

Take an interesting photo journey as you read about the ghost stories and sightings at many of Baltimore's haunted historical sites.

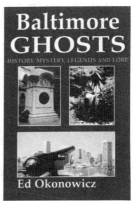

Learn about:

- Eerie events inside the Edgar Allan Poe House
- The Legend of 'Black Aggie'
- Spirits aboard the *USS Constellation*
- Ghosts that roam throughout Fells Point
- A young girl who haunts Route 40
- Frank the Body Snatcher's grave robbing
- Activity in Westminster Hall's Catacombs
- The Legend of the 'Poe Toaster'
- A ghostly musician in a haunted theater
- Several fascinating Tombstone Tales ... and more

136 pages
5 1/2" x 8 1/2"
softcover
ISBN 1-890690-13-9
$11.95

Includes more than 60 photographs of well-known Baltimore sites.

TEACHERS
Help your students learn and enjoy *history by using 'Baltimore GHOSTS' in your classroom.*

Our *Baltimore GHOSTS and HISTORY Teacher's Guide* includes graphic organizers, exercises, vocabulary, reproducibles, and activities that are ideal for immediate use in your classroom.

8 1/2" x 11"
$8.95

Created by Cassandra Cogan, an 8th grade special education teacher, this guide helps teachers focus on history while keeping students entertained and interested.

Visit our web site at: www.mystandlace.com

Lighthouse Legends, History and Lore

Lighthouses of New Jersey and Delaware
by Bob Trapani Jr.

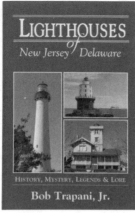

128 pages
5 1/2" x 8 1/2"
softcover
ISBN 1-890690-15-5
$11.95

Shipwrecks, storms, suicides, rescues, ghost stories, unusual events and regional folklore are featured in this unique coastal history of the mid-Atlantic region. Bob Trapani Jr., executive director of the American Lighthouse Foundation, presents lighthouse history in an entertaining and storytelling fashion using historic and contemporary photographs, oral history, document research and personal experiences. From Sandy Hook to Cape May and from Fenwick Island through the Delaware Bay enjoy tales of that offer history in an entertaining fashion.

Lighthouses of Maryland and Virginia
by Bob Trapani Jr.

Stories about light keepers and lighthouses of the Chesapeake Bay and Atlantic Coast are featured in this entertaining volume by lighthouse historian Bob Trapani Jr. From Assateague Island to Baltimore's Inner Harbor, from the Susquehanna Flats to the Virginia Coast enjoy stories about the region's magical and mystical lights. **Available Summer 2006.**

$11.95

Virginia's
Assateague Lighthouse

Maryland's
Thomas Point Lighthouse

Terrifying Tales of the Beaches and Bays
Volumes 1 and 2

In *Terrifying Tales of the Beaches and Bays* and the sequel, award-winning author and storyteller Ed Okonowicz shares eerie accounts of spirits roaming the mid-Atlantic beaches and shore.

Read about:

- A river pilot's memorable New Year's Eve cruise
- Desperate Confederates escaping from an island prison
- Serious seekers of hidden pirate gold
- Fishermen stranded in the icy Chesapeake Bay
- Lighthouse keepers still tending a long-gone beacon
- Ghosts at the Delaware Life Saving Station
- The Legend of Bigg Lizz
- and much more . . . .

$9.95 each

Ed Okonowicz

128 pages
5 1/2" x 8 1/2"
softcover
ISBN 1-890690-06-6

Ed Okonowicz

128 pages
5 1/2" x 8 1/2"
softcover
ISBN 1-890690-10-4

$6.95

Treasure Hunting
by Eddie Okonowicz

Dig up your own hidden treasures with this excellent "how to" book

This book is loaded with tips on using a metal detector to hunt for relics and treasure, plus photos of numerous historical finds.

True
Ghost Stories
from Master Storyteller
Ed Okonowicz

$\mathcal{S}$*pirits*
Between the Bays
Series

Wander through the rooms, hallways and dark corners of this eerie collection.

Creep deeper and deeper into terror, and learn about the area's history in our series of ghostly tales and folklore from states in the Mid-Atlantic region.

For detailed information on each volume, visit our web site

$9.95 each

"If this collection doesn't give you a chill, check your pulse, you might be dead."
    –Leslie R. McNair
    The Review, University of Delaware

"This expert storyteller can even make a vanishing hitchhiker story fresh and startling."
    –Chris Woodyard
    author of *Haunted Ohio* series

POSSESSED OBJECTS PLAGUE THEIR OWNERS

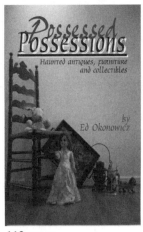

112 pages
5 1/2" x 8 1/2"
softcover
ISBN 0-9643244-5-8

Read about them in *Possessed Possessions* and *Possessed Possessions 2* the books some antique dealers **definitely** do not want you to buy.

A BUMP. A THUD. MYSTERIOUS MOVEMENT. Unexplained happenings. Caused by What? Venture through this collection of short stories and discover the answer. Experience 20 eerie, true tales about items from across the country that, apparently, have taken on an independent spirit of their own—for they refuse to give up the ghost.

From Maine to Florida, from Pennsylvania to Wisconsin—these haunted heirlooms exist among us—everywhere.

112 pages
5 1/2" x 8 1/2"
softcover
ISBN 0-890690-02-3

$9.95 each

"If you're looking for an unusual gift for a collector of antiques, or enjoy haunting tales, this one's for you."
—Collector Editions

"This book is certainly entertaining, and it's even a bit disturbing."
—Antique Week

". . . an intriguing read."
—Maine Antique Digest

Ed appeared on *Possessed Possessions*, an Antique Roadshow-type program filmed on the *Queen Mary*, and aired on The Learning Channel in 2005.

Disappearing Delmarva

Portraits of the Peninsula People

Photography and stories
by Ed Okonowicz

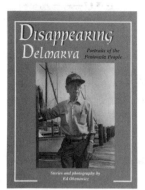

Disappearing Delmarva introduces you to more than 70 people on the peninsula whose professions are endangered. Their work, words and wisdom are captured in the 208 pages of this hardbound volume, which features more than 60 photographs.

Along the back roads and back creeks of Delaware, Maryland, and Virginia—in such hamlets as Felton and Blackbird in Delaware, Taylors Island and North East in Maryland, and Chincoteague and Sanford in Virginia—these colorful residents still work at the trades that have been passed down to them by grandparents and elders.

208 pages
8 1/2" x 11"
Hardcover
ISBN 1-890690-00-7

$38.00

Friends, Neighbors & Folks Down the Road

Photography and stories by
Ed Okonowicz & Jerry Rhodes

From small towns and villages in Lancaster County, Pa., Cecil County, Md., and New Castle, Kent and Sussex counties in Delaware, there are dozens of unique, surprising and entertaining characters waiting to be discovered in the stories and nearly 150 photographs in this book. They all prove that there are fascinating people worth knowing about, who are located right down the road and around the bend.

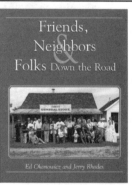

208 pages
8 1/2" x 11"
Hardcover
ISBN 1-890690-12-0

$30.00

"... fun-to-read coffee-table book"
—*Delaware Today Magazine*

"*Reading the first chapter is like finding a $20 bill in the pocket of your jeans on laundry day; unexpected, a pleasant surprise, an omen of good things to come.*"
—David Healey, *The Cecil Whig*

The DelMarVa Murder Mystery series

FIRED!

WELCOME

Ed
Okonowicz

320 pages
4 1/4" x 6 3/4"
softcover
ISBN 1-890690-01-5

$9.95

Early in the 21st century, DelMarVa, the newest state in the union, which includes Delaware and the Eastern Shore of Maryland and Virginia, is plagued by a ruthless serial killer. In *FIRED!* meet Gov. Henry McDevitt, Police Commissioner Michael Pentak and State Psychologist Stephanie Litera as they track down the peninsula's worst killer since 19th century murderess Patty Cannon.

to the
State of
DelMarVa

"Politics and romance make fairly strange bedfellows, but add a dash of mystery and mahem and the result can be spectacular, as evidenced in FIRED!"
—Sharon Galligar Chance
BookBrowser Review

"Lots of familiar places in this imaginative suspense novel."
—Jeannine Lahey
About.com
Wilmington, Del.

". . . this is Okonowicz's best book so far!"
—*The Star Democrat*
Easton, Md.

Halloween House

320 pages
4 1/4" x 6 3/4"
softcover
ISBN 1-890690-03-1

$9.95

In *Halloween House*, the series continues as Gov. McDevitt, Commissioner Pentak and other DelMarVa crime fighters go up against Craig Dire, a demented businessman who turns his annual Halloween show into a real-life chamber of horrors.

"Halloween House
*mystery chills
summer heat.*"
—Rosanne Pack
Cape Gazette

"Looking at the front cover, the reader knows it's going to be a bumpy night."
—Erika Quesenbery
The Herald

Visit our web site at: www.mystandlace.com

To complete your collection. . .
or to tell us about your ghostly experience, use the form below:

Name _____

Address_____

City_____State_____Zip Code_____

Phone _(_____)_____e-mail:_____

To receive the free *Spirits Speaks* newsletter and information on future volumes, public tours and events, send us your e-mail address, visit our web site [www.mystandlace.com] or fill out the above form and mail it to us.

I would like to order the following books:

Quantity	Title	Price	Total
_____	**Civil War Ghosts at Fort Delaware**	**$11.95**	_____
_____	Baltimore Ghosts	$11.95	_____
_____	Baltimore Ghosts Teacher's Guide	$ 8.95	_____
_____	**Lighthouses of Maryland and Virginia**	**$11.95**	_____
_____	Lighthouses of New Jersey and Delaware	$11.95	_____
_____	Terrifying Tales of the Beaches and Bays	$ 9.95	_____
_____	Terrifying Tales 2 of the Beaches and Bays	$ 9.95	_____
_____	Treasure Hunting	$ 6.95	_____
_____	Pulling Back the Curtain, Vol I	$ 8.95	_____
_____	Opening the Door, Vol II (second edition)	$ 9.95	_____
_____	In the Vestibule, Vol IV	$ 9.95	_____
_____	Presence in the Parlor, Vol V	$ 9.95	_____
_____	Crying in the Kitchen, Vol VI	$ 9.95	_____
_____	Up the Back Stairway, Vol VII	$ 9.95	_____
_____	Horror in the Hallway, Vol VIII	$ 9.95	_____
_____	Phantom in the Bedchamber, Vol IX	$ 9.95	_____
_____	Possessed Possessions	$ 9.95	_____
_____	Possessed Possessions 2	$ 9.95	_____
_____	Ghosts	$ 9.95	_____
_____	Fired! A DelMarVa Murder Mystery (DMM)	$ 9.95	_____
_____	Halloween House (DMM#2)	$ 9.95	_____
_____	Disappearing Delmarva	$38.00	_____
_____	Friends, Neighbors & Folks Down the Road	$30.00	_____
_____	Stairway over the Brandywine, A Love Story	$ 5.00	_____

*Md residents add 5% sales tax.
Please include $2.00 postage for the first book, and 50 cents for each additional book.
Make checks payable to:
    Myst and Lace Publishers

Subtotal_____

Tax*_____

Shipping _____

Total _____

All books are signed by the author. If you would like the book(s) personalized, please specify to whom.   Mail to: Ed Okonowicz
1386 Fair Hill Lane
Elkton, Maryland 21921

Visit our web site at: www.mystandlace.com